PRAISE FOR
KNOW

"In your hands you hold a blueprint to finding your way back to you. Keep this book within arm's reach and refer to it often. With Amy's guidance, you can live life on your terms and become the person you were always meant to be."

—**MARK LEBLANC**, CSP, CPAE, author of *Never Be the Same*

"A brave and soulful book . . . the permission slip you need to do things your way."

—**LITERARY TITAN**, Gold Book Award winner

"*Know* exposes the hidden costs of conformity and fear, sharing a raw, transformative journey to reclaim intuition, self-trust, and the freedom to live one's life by their own expression and therefore on their terms. A must-read for all women."

—**SARAH FISCHER**, MSW, MAHS, PhD, survival behavioralist

AMY CERNY VASTERLING

KNOW

Where the Status Quo Ends
and **YOU** Come to Life

RIVER GROVE
BOOKS

Throughout the book, I use stories from my own life, clients' lives, and from the experiences of people I've met along the way to illustrate points and concepts. The stories from my own life are relayed as faithfully as my memory allows, with full acknowledgment that others might remember events differently. When writing about clients and others beyond my immediate family, I have taken the liberty of changing names and some details in order to protect their privacy.

Published by River Grove Books
Austin, TX
www.rivergrovebooks.com

Distributed by River Grove Books

Design and composition by Greenleaf Book Group
Cover design by Greenleaf Book Group

Publisher's Cataloging-in-Publication data is available.

Print ISBN: 978-1-966629-14-6

eBook ISBN: 978-1-966629-15-3

First Edition

*This book is dedicated to all of the dreamers,
observers, and wise sensitive people,
including my children Jane and Peter.*

CONTENTS

Introduction 1

SECTION ONE: A World of Doubt

Chapter One Where Did You Go? 11

Chapter Two Our Model Lives. 19

Chapter Three The Way to You: Personal Knowing 31

SECTION TWO: Reclaiming Your Knowing

Chapter Four You Already Know. 45

Chapter Five Trust: Knowing's Active Ingredient. 57

Chapter Six Resistance-Free Living 73

SECTION THREE: Living in the Know

Chapter Seven You Are Your Teacher 89

Chapter Eight Relationship Evolution 111

Chapter Nine Keeping the Knowing Flowing 129

Acknowledgments 139

About the Author 141

INTRODUCTION

For much of my life, I felt as if there was a certain way to do things that others knew about but I did not—some secret to life I hadn't figured out. Throughout my childhood and well into my adulthood, I felt I was "doing life wrong" even though I was living a life people work hard to have and many people would have envied. I had a college degree, a husband, two children, a home we owned, and work that not only paid me a bit but also allowed me to contribute to the well-being of individuals and society. Still, I spent a lot of time and energy second-guessing everything I did, said, and chose. I spent a lot of time questioning myself. I never felt completely at ease in my body or in my life. The older I got, the worse it became. I felt disconnected from the way I was living, from many of the people in my life, and from myself. Yet at the same time, I undeniably knew myself. But when I'd daydream about doing things differently—maybe heading in a direction that would be considered out of the norm for a person like me—when I thought about having different kinds of people in my life, or when I felt sure somehow that I was meant for more and so there must be more out there for me—I'd quickly, almost automatically, admonish myself as selfish and ungrateful for all I did have in my life right now. After decades of this back-and-forth in my head, the discomfort of it became so constant and unbearable that I made a decision to stop trying to discard my thoughts, feelings, and growing agitation outright. I decided to be willing to be uncomfortable, to face it, and see what it might have to tell me.

In time, what came to me was that there was no hidden secret to life that I was missing. The cause of my distress was a lifetime of trying to suppress, and let's be honest, shut off and out that voice inside me—the one that held wisdom unique to me, the one that held my power and could direct me to a life where I would be fully me, the voice I would come to call my "personal knowing." By ignoring this voice—this personal knowing—I was all but ensuring I fell into a life that satisfied what others expected of me, not a life I wanted for myself, not the life I was born to live, not a life I found satisfying. The result was my nearly constant discomfort. I also started to see there was nothing unusual about what I was experiencing. In searching for answers to how I got to where I was and why I tried to stifle that inner voice at every turn, I talked with anyone who was open to a discussion about it. Through those conversations, I found that many people shared the same struggles and were asking the same questions.

Encouraged by our culture, many of us look outside ourselves for some guaranteed system for navigating our lives. We look for rules, directions, approval, permission—anything or anyone to take away the burden of having to make our own choices and being judged for it. The result is we live our whole life in pursuit of what others want for us or what our culture asserts we should want. We work to live as best we can within the constraints of a hierarchy. I call these man-made systems "The Model." Our dependence on this mode of operation leaves us forever unsure and insecure because we are always waiting on others to tell us who we are and what to do next. While we are attracted to The Model for the certainty it seems to promise, the lack of trust in ourselves it demands from us—lack of trust to know what's best for us—causes us to live in a state of uncertainty and fearfulness of our future. It leaves us powerless to direct our own lives, to tell ourselves who we are, and to choose to live as we feel called to.

When on occasion we do hear our own voice telling us to go a different way to discover what's truly possible for us, we doubt that voice, especially if it is encouraging us to do something outside The Model's parameters. Instead of following our knowing, we argue with it. And then we make sure whatever it has to say never reaches full expression through us. It is a confining and uncomfortable way to exist.

Adding to this pressure to conform, as a world, I believe we are living at the top edge of an extended narcissistic period in human history. In myriad ways, our culture conditions us to want to "win" at this game called life. On the surface, The Model causes a false sense of belonging within us and flimsy relationships for us based on outmoded ideals. Our religions and societies may tout messages of fellowship, charity, and cooperation over conflict, but the rules they lay down for us to follow drive us more toward a good-versus-evil, right-versus-wrong, and me-against-you mindset.

And yet, no one is winning. We live under the perception that control is power—while our lived experience tells us that nothing could be further from the truth. Control is control—and by definition, it steals our power from us. Still, these terms are often used interchangeably in conversation, giving more weight to this misconception and causing more confusion. In a world run by this ethos and by The Model—which ensures individuals find it difficult to have the sense of self or safety necessary to express who they are—both the individual and the world lose out.

People like me—and I am guessing you, since you picked up this book—sense this imbalance in what we know and how we live, even if we can't name it. It is the seed of our persistent agitation and anxiety. Even when we don't quite grasp what's going on, we feel the world is off-kilter. But not knowing why we feel this way or what to do about it, we settle back into the way things are. We buy into the belief that maybe this is just the way people are, the way cultures work, the way life works. There was I time I bought in to this too, a time when I told myself to believe in and live by The Model.

BREAKING DOWN TO BREAK FREE

Thankfully, my personal knowing wasn't going to let me rest there. And yours won't either. Never identified as handling repression well, my knowing's constant presence in the back of my head—and the constant discomfort that caused—were nudging me to let go of the uncertainty of looking to an outside authority to define me. It was telling me that if I wanted the life I was born to have and live out my full potential, I had to relearn to listen to and trust in my knowing.

This book contains what I learned on exploring how to follow that knowing and the wisdom I gathered along the way. I followed my knowing to start living a life that felt truer to me. In my professional capacity as an intuitive and advisor to predominantly highly sensitive people (a term we'll explore in upcoming chapters), I also wanted to illuminate this issue so others who are suffering as I had been might see themselves in my struggles, understand what is causing those struggles, and see there is a way to relieve their discomfort—as well as a more authentic life that is within their power to have. Beyond myself and my clients, I wanted my children to understand the importance of going the distance to reclaim our knowing and of working toward the full expression of ourselves, which is our birthright. I wanted them to see that having the courage to make the choices and follow through on what you know is worth it, even when it is hard. For all these reasons, I have dedicated myself for more than two decades to both researching personal knowing and living by it.

I have always understood this voice—my personal knowing—is louder in me than in most people. However, that doesn't mean it was easier for me to listen to it when it was prodding me to do things that made no obvious sense in the conventional world I was living in. Though often I could hear it loud and clear, I didn't quite know what to do about it. I often felt stuck and aching to make a move all at the same time. It is always scary to commit to listening to yourself—with no expert or cultural norm backing you up. This is even more true when what you know is telling you to veer away from what's expected, to color outside the lines, to risk being rejected, or worse in our culture, being wrong.

Over time, I came to regard this stuck feeling as a signal that Model-following me was breaking down. And with experience, I came to trust that by allowing and accepting this breaking down, I would change in the most favorable ways. My knowing showed me that as a world, we are moving past our greatest expression being a spiritual expression into our greatest expression being a human one. One by one, we are leaving The Model's patterns to clinch patterns more personal to us, the patterns of our knowing.

WRITING IT DOWN

In my own process to reconnect to and restore my knowing, I looked inward and challenged everything I had ever been told or assumed. I have had to confront my own demons, worries, and self-judgment, as well as fight off condemnation from others. I have lost friends. I have gained friends. I have found my way to trusting in me all over again. I have found my way to standing in my knowing on my own—allowing me to mature as an adult woman, mentally and emotionally. I have found my way to a life I feel good in, one I believe in, and that's mine. This process reflects how I'm built. It is mine. While the information in this book will help you understand and reconnect with your knowing, your journey to that knowing and the restoration of your power will be unique to you. To give you the clearest understanding of your personal knowing and what reconnecting to it means for your life moving forward, I've divided this book into three sections.

The chapters in the first section—A World of Doubt—explore how we get separated from our knowing in the first place, what that looks and feels like in our modern-day lives, and how this separation continues to promote disconnection throughout our lives. The first few chapters also explain how and why our innate need for certainty and security has left us feeling anxious, unrealized, and uncertain. Then, explicit and in-depth explorations of both personal knowing and The Model help you to understand the challenge here fully—so you can better see the solution. The section concludes with an exploration of the consequences of continuing to live in The Model. It also makes sure we know that the remedy to those consequences is our personal knowing, and it is waiting for us.

Section Two—Reclaiming Your Knowing—starts by making clear how to identify your personal knowing and what reclaiming it might look like and feel like. While reminded that your experience will always be unique to you, the chapters in this section help you understand that we all already know, that our knowing is and has always been with us, and how we are coerced by The Model to discount and suppress it. Further, you come to see how and why self-trust is the active ingredient that paves the way for our freedom from The Model and to permit our knowing to do the work only it can do for us. The chapters illuminate what the experience of being guided by our knowing looks like, how it relieves fear and worry, allows us to gain real wisdom through natural consequences, and encourages our growth.

The third and final section—Living in the Know—shows you that only you can reconnect yourself to your knowing. You are your best teacher. The chapters also give you insight into what life is like when knowing is your guide. You come to see how the daily challenges of our lives naturally fall away when we are guided by our knowing, replaced by an ease in living. You also see some of the difficulties you might experience as you move away from The Model and into your own knowing. You learn what you can expect, what to watch out for, and how to stay true to yourself and your knowing when things get tough.

Throughout the book, I use stories from my own life, clients' lives, and from the experiences of people I have met along the way to illustrate points and important concepts. The stories from my own life are relayed as faithfully as my memory allows, with full acknowledgment that others might remember events differently. When writing about clients and others beyond my immediate family, I have taken the liberty of changing names and some details in order to protect their privacy.

KNOW FOR YOURSELF

I do want to stress that this is not a "how-to" book. Again, your effort to reconnect with your knowing will be yours and yours alone. That said, I do hope that in every page you see that you are not alone in how you feel now or what you feel as you get closer to your knowing and re-establishing your true self. I believe we are moving out of that narcissistic period and entering another age. I believe something new is rising in the human experience, and the current Model is well on its way to becoming a relic. I see a greater pattern of humanity built from each person's knowing, a time when we live our lives as an art form with the primary purpose of our expansion as individuals, and so as a collective. I'm looking forward to living in that world. Those of us reconnecting to our knowing now are at the head of the curve and leading the way there by example.

My personal knowing is the truest, wisest, and most dependable guide in my life. Without it, I'd still be living out each day agitated, disliking myself and my life, and not understanding why. By trusting in my personal knowing, fear, doubt, and worry are no longer part of my everyday experience. I live with confidence in my choices and the peace that comes with the certainty of knowing that I am always where I need to be, doing what I am meant to be doing.

By extricating yourself from the conventional patterns of The Model and making room for your knowing to guide you, you make it possible to expand to your fullest potential. You'll not only find a stronger connection to yourself but also to others in your life and the world around you. Everything you need to make this happen, you have inside you right now. You can start today. Just turn the page.

—Amy

P.S. If you find this book speaks to you and would like to explore living through your knowing further, I invite you to join me and others working to reconnect to their knowing. To learn more go to www.amyvasterling.com.

Section One

A WORLD
OF DOUBT

Chapter One

WHERE DID YOU GO?

Most of us want to live a dynamic human experience—one that gives us access to the deepest expression of who we are, one that strengthens our natural connection to the world around us, to others, and to ourselves. We are born with a natural drive to live such a life, our life. And we are born with the knowledge that can guide us there.

We are also born into a world of responsibilities and expectations that force our disconnection from what is and from what we know. As children, we are regularly told to suppress, ignore, compromise, get on with it. Rarely, if ever, are we told to pay attention to ourselves, to feel, to sense, to let be. As a result, we live with fear, worry, and guilt about not measuring up, about missing out. At the same time, we feel over-extended—physically, mentally, and emotionally. We learn to dread being wrong. We want desperately to be right. (Much of the world is ill-governed on that string of words alone.)

So we busy ourselves with this modern life—living within a set of rules and expectations put in place by others long before we joined the human race. As we strive to fit in and achieve in this structure, we encounter both subtle and overt experiences that pit us against our nature while slowly extinguishing our inclinations. Our choice becomes to either live as someone we're not or to spend energy and focus fighting against society's insurmountable momentum. The continual tension is exhausting, leaving us constantly overthinking to solve our predicament. Most of us eventually give in to "the way things are." We focus so intensely on doing things "the right way" that we dismiss any leaning toward or trust in doing things our way.

When you take an honest look at how you got to where you are in your life right now, you see you have been driven there by others' expectations and the desire for certainty to make the "right" choices or the least risky ones anyway. You likely find yourself with a safe job, a safe relationship, a safe life—the things you were told would give you a good life but instead feel all wrong. Feeling conflicted, defeated, and overly sensitive, you can't help but wonder: "What happened to me? Where did I go?" You long for something else, something different, something that's just beyond your ability to verbalize. Yet, when you do entertain what that something else might be and how you might go after it, you shut it down. You conclude it is best to keep it away. You long to reconcile yourself with the world and to feel right in it, though a lifetime of lived experience makes you wonder if that is even possible.

It is possible. There is a path away from this life you are spinning in—a path toward living as who you are and are meant to be. It begins with tapping into that sense you've been trying to ignore—your knowing—and instead relearning to access and to trust in it. When you allow that personal knowing to guide you, you live the life you were meant for, one that grounds you in self-confidence, frees you from fear and worry, and re-establishes the connection you seek to the way your unique life was intended to be lived and create a life as you want to live it.

WE GET SEPARATED FROM OUR KNOWING

The message society feeds us, however, is that we don't know what is best for ourselves, that it is smarter and more certain—and so much safer—to trust in sources outside ourselves. As toddlers, we get rules to follow. Though we are still given the space to express our individual selves for the most part, we are dependent on parents who want to protect us and so encourage us to adhere to "the way things should be done" as soon as possible. By the time we hit eight or nine years old, our autonomy is looked down on, not trusted. Our potential becomes defined by how well we conform. Outside pressures teach us to suppress our knowing instead of expressing it.

With each year of our life, we put more distance between us and our knowing. We find the only way to shine is to listen to directions from sources outside ourselves and fall in line. And the only way to fall in line is to ignore our inner voice, our intuition, our own power. In time, our knowing is no longer easy to access. We start to doubt ourselves. We question our abilities, how we look, our aims in life. We force ourselves to do things we don't want to do—fearing if we do take a risk and fail, then what? We push ourselves to be someone we're not. Without our inner voice, we are unsure, and so we are stuck. Outside forces—our parents, our culture, our religion's dogma—take over the trajectory of our lives.

But ignoring knowing no longer sits well inside us. We are in a changing time, and much of our strife is caused by ignoring this part of us, our nature. Even when we are unaware of why we're doing things another's way, it feels unnatural because it *is* unnatural—and it causes problems in our lives. Depression and anxiety, to be sure. But also aggression. Some people break down physically, some mentally, some both. Most never really understanding why. Some just find themselves frustrated in an endless loop, telling themselves they are moving ahead, only to keep ending up in the same place.

HSPS: HIGHLY SENSITIVE PEOPLE

Because you consciously still feel your knowing and feel the desire to act on it—though you may have yet to do so—you likely are part of the 15–20 percent of the population known as highly sensitive people (HSPs).[1] Exceptionally attuned to their surroundings, HSPs are unable to fully suppress that voice inside them, no matter how much they try to conform to cultural norms.

I think of us HSPs as the elephants of human beings. Elephants are the epitome of knowing. They sense and remember. Because they can feel the truth of what has happened before and recognize the pattern in what is happening in the moment, they are able to determine what is coming. In other words, their knowing results in their being intuitive. And when they sense something is wrong, they start running, pounding the ground. This signals ground-based animals. They also trumpet with their trunks. This signals all the animals in the trees and sky. They get every creature to high ground as the flood comes or to safety as the earthquake rumbles.

When we human beings are attuned to our knowing, we too sense the truth and pattern of what is going on, whether positive, negative, or neutral. Like elephants, we yearn to signal what we know to protect and inform others. Further, because we sense the full picture, we can

---

1   The Highly Sensitive Person, https://hsperson.com.

better see solutions that work for all. Thus, what is good for us HSPs is good for everyone.

However, unlike the elephant and their fellow creatures in the wild, many of our fellow creatures in our civilized society have been desensitized to listening to their surroundings. So as an HSP, you likely have found yourself speaking the truth that nobody wants to acknowledge, seeing potential nobody wants to strive for, and pointing out opportunities no one wants to claim. Also likely, you are expressing what you know may have made other family members, your teachers, and co-workers uncomfortable. That's why most of us HSPs—and maybe you, too—learn to keep what we know or sense to ourselves.

Living this incongruity sometimes causes us HSPs to experience emotional and behavioral issues, usually starting in childhood. When we are young children (ages five to seven), this suppression can manifest as aggressive behavior or retreating altogether from other people. By the time we reach the age of eight or nine—about the time cultural expectations around gender roles begin to place limitations on us— we can present with anxiety, depression, or self-destructive behaviors. Unenlightened parents or guardians tend to respond to such symptoms by encouraging more conformity in their HSP children—which only exacerbates our frustration and thus our reactions.

In your own childhood, this systemic paving over your personal knowing likely caused you to lose touch with who you are, what you know, and how to operate in life's flow. The result is you find yourself in adulthood "going along to get along," yet always feel something is wrong. That's because this is not who you are and not the life you were built for or meant to live.

As an HSP child myself, I too learned to suppress what I thought, felt, and knew. As I grew—like most female members of my generation—I learned to keep the peace, compromise in my relationships, and convince myself to settle for less than I wanted, less than what I knew to be possible for my existence. When I did ask for what I needed, if those requests were pushed away or unacknowledged, I acquiesced—and moved further away from who I was and am.

By first grade, for instance, I was already being forced to capitulate to authority. Teachers wanted me—and all students—to learn the way they wanted us to learn. Most teachers didn't have bad intentions. They believed getting their students to follow instructions, to do it the way the teachers themselves had learned to, was the best way to educate all children. So when I looked out the window instead of focusing on a test, when I changed the story in the reader to make my own (and I thought better) ending, when I spoke up—when I did not conform—I was rebuffed, corrected, and instructed to do as I'd been told. In other words, I was shut down, as was my curiosity and desire to be in class. In time, I stopped speaking. Because I wasn't enthusiastic, I was soon labeled by the powers that be as "challenging" (not a positive term in that era). To this day, I wonder what my school career might have been like if I'd found more compassion, encouraged curiosity, and room for self-expression in class. I wonder what kind of love for school might have been instilled in me and other "challenging" students—and what was lost to us and to the world because of the rigidity drilled into our teachers.

What I learned in school was reinforced at home, in church, and in my relationships. In my childhood home, children had a place; parents were right at all costs. Kids were seen not as individuals but as a commodity, of sorts, who all thought and felt the same, and so should be treated the same. This was not unusual at that time. Many of us were brought up in households where a parent's highest aim was to get their children to behave—"don't cry," "don't talk back," "don't get out of line." We were to fit into the hierarchy of society as it had been constructed for us. We were not to ask questions or be emotional. Even today, force, shame, and control are ever present in the way adults think they are supposed to relate to children—and each other.

As an intuitive reader and advisor to predominantly highly sensitive people, I have spent the last twenty years studying that tension between following the constraints that the hierarchy sets out for us—which I call "The Model"—and our personal knowing. I have helped thousands of clients reconcile their relationships with pressures that cause them to disconnect from The Model and reconnect to themselves, to their knowing, in order to live out the full potential of who they were meant to be.

RECLAIMING YOUR KNOWING

While silencing my inner voice—my knowing—was a useful survival tactic in my early life and a way to keep the peace as an adult, it did not change how I felt or what I knew. The same goes for you. You already know what is true for you. You know what action to take, what to do next. It is time now for your knowing to resurface in your life.

Our lives can be far easier. We can relieve the doubt and second-guessing that makes us suffer. We can solve our challenges as they come, see our way forward with clarity, and—best of all—reestablish our connection to others and ourselves in the truest way. That's because feeling stuck in your life is the result of ignoring who you truly are, who you know yourself to be. Our nature as human beings is to flow in life. We must relearn to step back into our knowing, recapturing how to dream, to act on our curiosity, to reconnect to everything in a way that feels enlivening, and to experience being fully human.

I'm not pretending any of this is easy. But there is nothing harder than holding up a life filled with fear or suppression, a life that is disingenuous, a life that isn't really yours. It takes work to reclaim your knowing and live from your source of wisdom. Fortunately, everything you need for the journey is already within you. That I know.

Chapter Two

OUR MODEL LIVES

I was driving on a busy highway when a question popped into my head: *What does the woman in the car passing me want?* What? The next day I got a similar message: *What does my child's teacher want?* With that second question, I knew what these messages were telling me, and it struck a deep chord. We don't all strive for one way to live life, one way to qualify our idea of success. That is true.

However, what is also true is that most of us don't end up working toward our own way of living, our own definition of success. Let's be honest: we often don't make room for others in our lives—like our children, our spouses—to work toward theirs either. Most of us default to The Model that I mentioned in the last chapter for how to live—a set of rules and expectations handed down to us by our parents and culture, and then almost unconsciously handed off by us to our own offspring and those in our community.

SOCIETY IS A KIND OF CULT

In the early twentieth century, industrialization was on the rise, and along with it, worker exploitation. While socialism and communism did gain in popularity (workers began to organize, and some significant revolutions did occur), the total toppling of the world economic order by workers (a prediction made by Karl Marx) didn't happen. Antonio Gramsci, an Italian intellectual and a founder of the Italian Communist Party, wondered why. Why did the underclass allow their own exploitation by those in power? His answer became the theory of hegemony.[2]

Now stay with me here. Though the term "hegemony" derives from the Greek meaning "domination," the theory proposes that the working class is not forced or even coerced to labor for low wages while enriching the elite. The concept of hegemony contends that people consent to being dominated, and that's why we rarely revolt in huge numbers.

This consent comes from our desire to live by the ideals of our culture—ideals that are introduced to us and then reinforced through the culture's language, stories, media, religion, school curriculum, and family life. People from all social classes in a culture accept, believe, and stick with these standards and expectations. Even more fascinating, all this occurs without anyone—the ruling class or the ruled—being particularly conscious of it. To most of us, it is "just the way things are." So much so that we regard our unchallenged assumptions as "common sense." In other words, we go against ourselves in an effort to believe we are connecting and, therefore, belonging. We put up with injustice to ourselves and others in order to secure our place in our society.

---

2   James Martin, "Antonio Gramsci," in *The Stanford Encyclopedia of Philosophy* (Spring 2023 Edition), eds. Edward N. Zalta and Uri Nodelman, first published January 13, 2023, https://plato.stanford.edu/archives/spr2023/entries/gramsci.

Gramsci concedes that tensions do arise from time to time between the haves and the have-nots, resulting in social unrest, protests, and strikes. When that happens, the powerful give a little (increasing wages, expanding voting rights, legalizing marijuana, or whatever) to keep the public content. But the foundational ideas that make up the fabric of the culture—and keep the elite in power—remain.

I'm not trying to give you a history or sociology lesson here. For our purposes, Gramsci's hegemony theory speaks to how deeply the norms of any society are embedded in the thought patterns of those who live in it—embedded so deeply we consider ideas as facts, and we allow them to go unexplored to the detriment of our knowing and to the quality of our lives.

KEEPING US IN LINE

"Hegemony" results in The Model—those rules and expectations we default to in our everyday lives. There are good, sensible reasons we comply with The Model. Sharing a group ideology allows for community—something human beings need. In addition, collectively accepted rules allow us to get along, so we can be more productive and secure than we could be by going it alone. The Model also pushes our very human buttons for certainty and belonging. It eliminates the gray areas of life. It provides us with a life plan and a moral code to live by. There's a real relief in knowing your place and what's expected of you.

But that is also what's wrong with it. The Model is confining. If those gray areas are not questioned and explored, they become limiting. If you scratch just a little on The Model's surface, you find it assumes a lot—to the detriment of individual and collective growth and advancement. For instance, in the United States, The Model tells us that "if we work hard and play by the rules," positive outcomes (positive, according to The Model anyway) are practically guaranteed. Of course, that Model also puts the responsibility for any failure on us—conveniently absolving the hierarchy and dismissing systemic problems The Model creates. If we refuse to see the real problems and don't question their true source, we can't do better and be better as individuals or as a society.

HIERARCHIES AND EXPECTATIONS

Not too long ago, I was volunteering in an elementary school classroom. The teacher introduced me as Mrs. Vasterling. When I rose to speak, I let the children know I prefer they call me Amy. I said it instinctually. It was what I wanted. Immediately, the teacher jumped up to correct me. She said, "I think what Mrs. Vasterling was trying to say is . . ." I interrupted. "No, I really would like it if they called me Amy." With that, she shot me an unpleasant look and sat back down behind her big desk.

Thinking about that teacher's reaction later, I realized what I'd done to upset her. Rightfully or wrongfully, mindfully or not, I stepped away from The Model with my request and disrupted her expectations, as well as the hierarchy of her classroom. In contrast, this teacher felt more comfortable following centuries of human practice and operating within The Model's hierarchy. However, such a practice crushes individual agency, identity, and self-worth. It limits our ability to have intimacy with others, to see within, and to have the generosity of mind to allow behavior that might be different from ours.

By definition, hierarchies declare one person or one way of doing things more valuable than another, which fuels The Model. Those seen as "lesser than" or who challenge the hierarchical authority often suffer unnaturally high consequences for any perceived break with The

Model. Those who noticeably pose a threat to the status quo are often jailed, mistreated, or even killed for straying—think Galileo, Martin Luther King Jr., Karen Silkwood, or Colin Kaepernick. The fascist government of dictator Benito Mussolini sentenced Gramsci to twenty years in prison (later commuted to twelve years) for his ideas. Gramsci fell ill in prison and died in a state sanatorium six days after completing his sentence.[3]

In contrast, those who live at the top of the hierarchy are usually protected from experiencing the natural consequences of their actions. While many might dismiss this as simply unfair, it is more insidious and far-reaching for all of us than that. Without experiencing natural consequences, a person doesn't learn and so does not mature. Because most of our leaders come from this protected rank and oversee the systems and make the rules, our culture doesn't mature—keeping it reactive, intolerant, unable to take an honest look at itself in order to solve its problems and advance. (This is exceptionally frustrating for HSPs, who can see a better way.) Additionally, diverse thought is prevented, restraining what's possible for us as a collective and limiting choices for all individuals, no matter our place in the hierarchy. We all know this. We all feel it in the limits placed on our lives. Yet, the majority of people stay in their place and do what's expected—suppressing their knowing and allowing the social pressures inherent in The Model to keep them in line.

If you asked that teacher why she objected to the children calling me by my first name, she'd likely have responded with a set of "common sense" reasons—all of which would adhere to The Model's definition of the relationship between children and adults. I'd also argue that in that moment, her mind didn't pause to consider whether students calling

---

3   Martin, "Antonio Gramsci."

an adult by their first name was okay. No, her thought process went straight to: What do I need to do to maintain the status quo here? And how do I get everyone back into their place (including Amy) within the classroom hierarchy? From her perspective, my request threatened chaos and maybe even deteriorating respect from her pupils—leaving her feeling desperate to bring it all back within the bounds of the culture's norm.

THE MODEL SEPARATES US FROM OUR KNOWING

The hierarchy—and the expectations accompanying it—are everywhere in our society. I'm sure you can easily identify the hierarchy in your own life, as well as your role within it—your family, your workplace, your religion, even your social group. Any role in the hierarchy comes with expectations we follow for ourselves and impose on everyone around us. We do this casually, over time, and without awareness—without thinking through the consequences to ourselves, our children, or society itself.

When we hold a baby in our arms or see a toddler at play, for instance, we can't help but muse about their future—who they'll be, what they'll achieve in their life. As we watch them engage with their world, we naturally envision them hitting all the milestones (a.k.a., expectations) The Model values—graduations, a good job, marriage, children, etc. We see them happy, safe, and living a fulfilling life, as we, our culture, and their place in the hierarchy define it for them. We become afraid if "all of a sudden" at age seven, they start having problems in school. The fear inside us as parents can become overwhelming and finding a solution to get them back on track can feel daunting. If this sounds like you—and let's face it, it sounds like most of us—it is a sign you are in The Model. There's an easier way.

Of course, we need to set some expectations for our lives or we wouldn't progress, we wouldn't discover what is possible for us. The key is to ensure those expectations aren't what someone else set for you, but that they support you and your knowing. For instance, my son loves math and was consistently achieving scores in the high nineties on his tests, which was great. Then, his father challenged him (set the expectation) to get 100 percent. And our son did it. This was a healthy expectation—not because our son hit the marker his dad set but because that marker reflected an achievement our son wanted for himself and therefore went after it. Also, he knew his father's love, approval, and belief in him were not dependent on him meeting that expectation. But getting that nudge from his dad, having an expectation based on what he wanted for himself, empowered our son to realize he was capable of more.

It is when emotions, absolutes, and approval come into play that The Model's hierarchy and its expectations can be a problem and drive anxiety, insecurity, and misery. A client came to me wanting to figure out how to handle an issue with her fourteen-year-old son. An adept baseball player, the child was having high levels of anxiety on the field—and it was only mid-season. The parents were divided about what to do. My client's husband was enraged by the thought that the child would be allowed to quit. My client, on the other hand, "knew" her son needed to quit. But she didn't trust her knowing because The Model agreed with her husband's stance.

According to The Model—and this is probably familiar to you—children need to finish what they start. The standard advice here would be that the boy doesn't have to play next season, but he does need to see this season through. That's common sense, right?

There most definitely are times in our lives when sticking it out teaches us good lessons—like being careful what we commit to in the first place, as well as the gifts of perseverance. These lessons can serve us well and are important to know. But sticking it out can also keep us stuck in a bad situation and not allow us to take advantage of a better opportunity, one in which we might grow and flourish in a direction that suits us better. Also, important to know: The Model can't tell us which situation is which; only our knowing can do that.

After introducing the mother to the idea of The Model and its expectations, she decided to break from the standard advice and trust in her knowing. She approached her son with an open mind and asked what he wanted, with no judgment, no expectation attached. Without hesitation, he said, "I feel I need to quit." Then she asked how he'd feel about that fifteen years from now. He thought, and then said, "I don't think I'll even remember it." To which she replied, "Then quitting is what you need to do." She added, "I want you to learn right now to trust what you feel, even if your dad and I cannot understand it at first. I don't want you to grow into an adult who stays in situations or around people that make you anxious or that you know are wrong for you. I want you to trust that you know what's best for you."

Dad, however, was not on board with his son's decision. Both the mother and the son tried to explain. With his mother's encouragement, the boy even wrote out why he felt the need to leave the team. But the father could not receive his son's message. He even went so far as to say to his son, "You'll always be a quitter."

This dad was stuck in The Model. Because the father's behavior was antithetical to what he really wanted for his son, it was obvious he'd become completely detached from his knowing, unable to tap into even the tiniest sense of it. By insisting his son finish out the season, this dad was not addressing his son's anxiety, which was the real problem here. He was undermining his son's burgeoning ability to use his own judgment. And he was hurling insults at his son that could result in psychological damage and the underachievement the dad so desperately wanted to avoid. All the while, he believed he was doing the "right" thing for his child. The Model led him astray.

This father couldn't see that every "should" he tried to impose on the situation moved him further from solving the issue and further from his family. Instead of changing his tack when he saw his way wasn't working, he doubled down and became more controlling. Thankfully, this kid had an enlightened mother who had enlightened support and could explain the dynamics here, so the child didn't carry his father's burden and would not pass it on to his own children.

AUTHORITARIAN CONTROL AND ENABLING

The behavior used to make someone conform to The Model is typically expressed in one of two ways—authoritarian control (what the dad was using on his son) or its more subtle cousin, enabling. Authoritarian control responds to a hurt child's cry by saying, "You're fine"—ignoring their pain and denying or avoiding their feelings altogether. Enabling is gushing over a child's small scrape in an effort to take their pain from them—preventing them from experiencing natural consequences and learning to self-manage pain and other hardships. Make no mistake: while enabling might look like caring and selflessness, it is just as calculating, restraining, and selfish as authoritarian control. Both come down to robbing others of their agency. Both say in their own way that the other person can't trust in themselves, so they need to trust in and rely on someone else. Both are also fueled by fear.

If The Model tells us there is a "right" way, we conclude there must be a "wrong" way. The need to control another—in whatever form that takes—is a reaction to fear of someone choosing the "wrong way." The controller is afraid the other person's choice might reflect on them and lead to losing status, feeling ashamed, being rejected, or whatever else The Model threatens us with. We do not see that the real threat is the unquenchable need to control and enable. When we are in the midst of acting on either, we don't ask questions, allow for answers, or see the reality of a situation. That father never made room to gently and with an open mind explore what might be causing his son's anxiety. We send the message to those we are trying to push back into The Model that they are not capable, while our true motivation is that we are afraid their choices will pull us outside The Model with them.

In the end, both forms of control are futile and only aim to sabotage us. All this certainty we think they can create for our lives is an illusion. The more we control and enable, the more we lose connection to and the power within our own life. Therefore, life becomes a Sisyphean effort to conform to The Model and demand others do the same. It is a lot of time and effort without advancing naturally in your own life, ever. The boulder rolls back down the hill, and your need to right the situation according to The Model calls you to push the rock back up over the hill again and again.

The antidote to this is knowing you are the only person you can know for and the only person you need to know for. You knew as a child, and if you allow it, you will know again as an adult for yourself.

WHY LIVING "RIGHT" FEELS SO BAD

While saying "yes" to The Model might feel like a relief in the moment, it becomes suffocating as we try to live it every day. (Likely, that's the feeling that motivated you to pick up this book.) Instead of a glide path through life, The Model becomes a cruel hoax. The connection it promises never arrives because the authenticity needed for true connection is never created. We are following a model, after all—not making choices and taking actions that are authentic to us. This is how a lifetime of doing everything right results in a life that feels all wrong. When we only see life from The Model's perspective, being our whole selves becomes nearly impossible.

Every time we default to The Model, we move further from checking in with ourselves. The Model's "shoulds" push our knowing out of the equation. Its "coulds" and "woulds" delay us from being honest about what we know to be true. It becomes harder and harder for us to discern what we really think about anything. We feel muddled and unclear. We wonder if it is even okay to have needs. We cannot stand up for ourselves because we feel powerless, and it feels dangerous to be vulnerable. The further we descend into The Model, the harder it becomes to hear our inner voice.

Those who live by The Model alone live constrained. They likely cannot see why but can feel something is wrong and see no way out. Instead of facing reality and dealing with it constructively, they work to force the circumstances of their lives into a set of rules. Eventually, The Model can only deliver a life of self-doubt that paralyzes their potential—making it that much harder to free themselves from the hierarchy. You might be able to play the game of The Model, but you will never win. And that doesn't feel good—to anyone.

To me, the costliest consequence of being separated from our knowing is in playing beneath our true talent. We wake up in the morning not to experience all this world has to offer but to seek assurance, prestige, and acceptance. We turn into a person The Model wants us to be, not who we are, not who we want to be. We spend our lives working toward a standard when we ourselves are not standard.

Chapter Three

THE WAY TO YOU: PERSONAL KNOWING

Bronnie Ware walked away from a successful, fifteen-year career in banking to pursue a life as a creative. While writing songs and working to define what being "a creative" would mean for her, she paid the bills with contract jobs. One was in palliative care. As she helped her infirm and mostly elderly clients through their days, many confided in her. They talked about their lives and their loved ones, and many shared their regrets. The more regrets Ware heard, the more she realized that while her clients' lives had been different, many of their regrets were the same. Most came down to wishing they had followed their heart and lived more instead of doing what was expected of them.

In those regrets, Ware found encouragement and a permission of sorts to keep going after the unconventional life she felt called to.

Thinking other people might benefit from that kind of permission, she posted an essay online in 2009 listing five of the most common regrets her clients expressed. That essay not only went viral, but it also became the seed for her 2012 memoir, *The Top Five Regrets of the Dying: A Life Transformed by the Dearly Departing*. As the book became an international best seller, translated into thirty-two languages, Ware found her place as a full-time creative.[4]

The common regrets Ware observed, like all regrets, are products of being disconnected from our knowing, of choosing to live by The Model rather than by our own expression of life. If we want to remove regret from our lives—to live instead with joy, knowing who we are, and with confidence in the future—we have to let go of The Model we're clinging to and embrace our personal knowing. Much like Ware did herself.

THE CONSEQUENCES OF IGNORING YOUR KNOWING

As we've discussed, many of us were raised by parents who followed The Model's hierarchal system when it came to child-rearing. Thus, whatever our parents said is what we children were expected to do and did. No discussion was allowed—discouraging any attempt we children made at learning to figure things out on our own.

One of my clients came from a home where her parents used their Model-given authority to pit their children against each other. Everything from their report cards to chores to what subject they brought up at the dinner table turned into a competition to win

---

4 Bronnie Ware, *The Top Five Regrets of the Dying: A Life Transformed by the Dearly Departing* (Hay House, 2019); Bronnie Ware, "Regrets of the Dying," https://bronnieware .com/regrets-of-the-dying.

their parents' approval, and through that, a momentary connection to them. The children were constantly fighting to gain top position. Following The Model made their home more like a war zone—a painful, confusing, and scary place for children to grow up. Like all children, they were dependent on their parents. Having to fight for security made these children insecure. It cut them off from their knowing and thus from their ability to mature into adults able to realize their full potential.

Though most childhoods aren't as perplexing, many of us still grew up in homes where "because I said so" was a familiar refrain. Following The Model (because being right is all they know to do), many parents struggle to see that their children follow the rules and meet expectations. Often, parents don't feel great about the actions they take to keep their children in line. They go against their better judgment. But they believe this is the way to prepare their children to survive in this world and maybe achieve a place in the upper tiers of the hierarchy. If a child falls short (and most of us HSPs fall short of this goal because we see the shallowness of it), the parents themselves often feel judged and unworthy, making the children feel this too.

When children hit adolescence, some begin to question their parents and The Model. My client certainly did. Most of the time when she confronted her parents, they discounted and snubbed her. However, in those few instances where she felt heard, she also felt a real and reciprocated connection with her parents—because in these instances, she'd broken through The Model. In those heated exchanges, both she and her parents spoke truth and so saw the truth of each other. But it never lasted long. As soon as her questions made her parents feel vulnerable, they'd dig in and quickly retreat to The Model and the shield against reality it provided. Sadly, that shield also prevented them from connecting with their children and themselves.

My client, however, says those few times she did experience connection with them were enough to reveal to her that something was not right in their family—and that when she was ready, she'd need to figure that out and make a break. Though she continued to play her role in her family dynamics and enable The Model, she did so knowing there was a better way, and she would eventually find it. Her ending up in my office was a step toward that.

Adherence to The Model does not create security for children or a sure future—nothing can do that. It creates a sense of chaos in the child's bond with their parents and thus, throughout the home. To survive in this environment, children have to ignore their knowing and live up to The Model as much as they can. They then enter adulthood unable to fully believe in themselves, their own judgment, and their worth as individuals. Though their knowing is still there nagging at them, their self-doubt has been allowed to gain strength. Their voice is still inside them, but they've learned not to use it because no one wants to hear it.

This parental undermining of a child's growing autonomy was and remains a common phenomenon in our society. The result is generation after generation of adults who are separated from their knowing and so never develop an inner compass, never trust in themselves. They become adults who are afraid to make decisions or take risks for fear of doing something "wrong" and losing an authority figure's approval or love. Even more consequential, because this style of parenting is all these children know, they go on to parent their own children the same way with The Model's assurance that they are doing the right thing. Or they parent in the exact opposite way—no rules—in rebellion. Either way, they fall into The Model—parenting by reaction, not from a place of true knowing what best meets their individual child's needs.

A WASTE OF ENERGY

When our lives become nothing more than meeting the expectations of others, we do ourselves and the world a disservice. In sessions with clients, I refer to this as "hoop-jumping"—jumping through another's expectation to meet an outcome you don't want for yourself. When we persist in becoming someone we are not, putting all our energies toward achieving a life we haven't chosen, we lose touch with our knowing, resulting in anxiety through attachment to outcome. This is a fool's errand and a waste of energy. Whenever you feel anxiety around any decisions you've made, you can rest assured it is The Model talking and telling you to meet someone else's expectation for you, which likely was an expectation once placed on them. In other words, someone is dumping their trauma on you and expecting you to carry it.

All of this has come about because your power is misplaced or misunderstood due to The Model—leaving you disconnected from your knowing and thus feeling lost in your own life. We misplace our power when we trade it for security and comfort. We find ourselves more focused on the result than the life we are living on our way there. Even if we end up with the "prize" The Model told us to strive for, we arrive there positioned incorrectly for who we are. Eventually, we become weighed down by fear and complacency. Cut off from our knowing, we feel stuck.

Similarly, and perhaps as a result of misplacement, our power becomes displaced when our lives or The Model force us onto a path we aren't drawn to. For instance, pursuing a major in college not because it interested you but because your parents wanted you to have something to "fall back on." Or staying with a job that bores you because it pays a good salary. Or any situation you just keep enduring. In these circumstances, we need to shift our power away from The Model's fear and toward our knowing, believing in ourselves alone, and putting us back in charge of our life.

We get stuck because when we are children our power is misunderstood. This is an epidemic in the United States. In fact, this misunderstanding is what creates the misplacement and displacement. If our needs are ignored when we are little, if our caregivers aren't truthful about what we as children are observing and maybe even stating, if the parents themselves are not mature and do not understand how to trust us instead of judging us as children, being misunderstood becomes a silent yoke impeding our natural ability to have agency in our own lives.

The only way to rebalance our lives—to stop jumping through hoops, come to a true understanding of our power, and regain the wisdom of our knowing—is to make our own Model-free choices. As I worked to rediscover my own knowing and found the courage to let go of The Model, I had to face a hard truth about my marriage of more than twenty years: I was staying in it to live up to others' expectations. I didn't want to disappoint anyone. Once I admitted to myself what I knew, rationalizing my predicament and searching for justifications to stay became more difficult and anxiety-producing with each day. I could see I was hoop-jumping and misplacing my power in a million different ways.

After a mutually agreed upon separation from my spouse, I slowly untethered myself from my Model-approved marriage. My personal knowing led me to realize that the marriage model my spouse and I had created together was only amplifying the insecurity bred in me by my family of origin. I faced the fact that for more than two decades, 90 percent of my life had been me enduring things that were not true to who I am. I knew I needed to get back to being me. I needed to trade in The Model—as well as all of my fear—and let go to my knowing.

I also realized that coming to the end of this marriage relationship was not a surprise for either of us, nor was it a failure. It was another step in the process of living fully in our knowing. All of these steps to release myself from The Model taught me what I needed to know to move closer to my true self and my true life. Something I hope each person who reads this book does in their own way. Once we stop using The Model to protect us, we find our way to trusting our knowing because it is a natural state for each of us.

THE POWER IN OUR KNOWING

A client of mine, Andrea, woke one morning feeling extra concern for her father, who was in a memory care facility. She quickly reconfigured her schedule for the day and headed over to see him. When she entered his room, she could see he was agitated. He'd heard some news on the TV about a kidnapped child and had convinced himself that his twelve-year-old son (her brother, who was now an adult) was caring for this child when she was kidnapped. He blamed his son for being so irresponsible as to let this happen. The whole notion was preposterous, of course. But such confusion and conflation are not unusual for someone suffering with dementia.

Andrea knew it did no good to argue with the dementia. So, she went along with the story but decided to add some details she knew would calm her father. She told him that her brother did the right thing by asking for help and reminded her father that her brother, himself, "was just a child." She added that the little girl had not only been found, but it turned out she had not been kidnapped. With that, Andrea's dad was visibly relieved and relaxed. Then, out of the blue, he said, "I never knew why we treated you kids so badly."

This was the first time Andrea had ever heard her father acknowledge how he had misjudged her and her siblings—always thinking the worst of them, leaving them feeling continually misunderstood. Throughout her childhood, he had been quick to punish, never bothering to ask what happened from their point of view. When Andrea was growing up, The Model expected parents—especially dads—to keep an emotional distance from their children. Parents were supposed to be feared by children. According to The Model, a father's job was to mete out punishment in order to maintain control.

But that morning, for an instant—and maybe only for that instant—Andrea's father questioned The Model's expectations for him and revealed his true self to his daughter, not through apology but through realization. Andrea got to witness him doubt The Model he had followed all his life and connect to his knowing. It was a small but profound shift and one that allowed for enough vulnerability so that Andrea found empathy for her father and thus, true connection to him for the first time in her life.

Just as important to acknowledge, by following her own knowing that day and changing her emotional pattern with her father (showing up for him and responding to him gently with compassion and wisdom instead of following The Model: "No, no, Dad; that isn't what happened."), Andrea allowed her father to access his knowing. This is the power of stepping away from The Model and following your knowing.

If we can overcome the fear of leaving The Model, knowing has the power to set things right in our lives. While it may seem like a simple thing to do once you are aware of it, it can be complex because we are so entangled in The Model. Even when we want to live by our knowing, we can remain unconsciously tied to The Model. True healing doesn't come with awareness alone or through a few decisions based on what we feel is our knowing. To clinch this takes change equal to the epic hurt that brought you away from what you know.

For many, it takes infirmity and approaching death to see The Model for what it is and what it has done to them—as both my client Andrea and Bronnie Ware witnessed. In general, it is not the easy things in life that finally get us to leave The Model and accept our knowing; it is the hard things, the painful things, the traumatic things that won't let us be comfortable within the status quo. For HSPs especially, staying in a distorted, controlled way is not an option. These things force us to question our situation and ourselves, desire change, and make us look beyond The Model.

Consider yourself lucky that the emotional pain and discomfort you've experienced inside The Model have become profound enough to make you want to address them. As you begin the process of leaving The Model behind and claiming your knowing, you can expect positive shifts in your life. For instance, your possibilities will expand. Acting from your knowing means no longer being limited by conventional thinking or hindered by The Model's weighty "shoulds." When you replace the fear of risk with the certainty of knowing, you become free to consider what you might have cast aside before. You decide what's next for you—not somebody else's ideas for you via The Model.

In addition, confidence replaces any insecurity. By leaning on your knowing and working with it, you see the potential in your dreams and let doubt go. You are no longer waiting on outside approval, no longer tied up in other people's opinions or societal trends. Decisions become easier to make, and the confidence in your choices makes moving forward less complicated.

Your knowing has the power to align every aspect of your life. While The Model pushes against the natural order, creating disorder that presents as a facade of control, knowing puts you in the flow of your life. You start to see situations are neither bad nor good. You accept change more freely because you understand only our fear holds us attached—fear that's been cultivated by The Model and imposed upon us by society as we also impose it on others. You may still get hurt sometimes. But the difference is you know you won't be stuck in that pain. You know you will move past it, and the future will take care of itself.

Naturally, in time, you come to trust in yourself, in what you know. The Model relies on our fear to push us into looking to it to provide guardrails for our life, though those guardrails often fail us, creating things we don't like. When you shift your perception, you quickly learn that your knowing is the only guardrail you need, the true starting point you can really count on. By using your knowing as a guiding force, in time, you'll learn to recognize and trust it.

With all this, you find that as you move toward who you are, people who champion your skills and believe in you enter your life, and people who want to keep you stuck in The Model fall away. Inner quiet and calm become your regular state of being—no practice needed. Chaos dissipates as your personal knowing delivers clarity. You recognize what information is valuable for you and what is not. You know what to hold on to and what to let go.

As a result, life becomes easier, even simple. You start feeling alive again, hopeful, and ready for what's next. For those of us who have had a steep journey in life, this won't be easy or quick. Your journey to restore your knowing is likely to be equal in difficulty to the trauma that silenced it. However, there are undeniable treasures in investing your energy in getting all the way out of The Model and into your knowing.

When we allow our knowing to guide us, actions in our lives once controlled by The Model are now done in freedom. Without the guilt and pressures of trying to live up to some arbitrary societal standard, self-judgment is lifted, and worry is replaced by curiosity. We no longer try to fit things into our lives that don't work or don't feel right for us. Guided by our knowing, our life reflects our values. Every part of us is integrated, which is the ultimate in self-expression. We have nothing to prove to anyone.

YOU ARE YOUR REMEDY

Know that our world is banking on our fear and insecurity to keep us in The Model, to keep us wanting to deceptively feel "in control," when all we're really doing is handing over our control to the hoops The Model sets in place for us. We surpass our fears by allowing ourselves to be vulnerable. The truth is there is nothing more powerful, nothing that feels more secure, than knowing who you are and acting on it. When we lead with our personal knowing, it sets positive change in motion. We receive so much more love and rightful autonomy.

When you know you have created your life in complete honesty, you also feel secure enough in the vulnerability of that to allow others in your orbit to be who they are. When you release yourself, you release others. In this way, you make way for everyone to be responsive to their lives—including you.

Section Two

RECLAIMING YOUR KNOWING

Chapter Four

YOU ALREADY KNOW

n 1950, a mother learned her nearly three-year-old daughter had a brain disorder. The child had yet to speak and was showing other signs of atypical mental development. The doctors recommended institutionalization—which was the conventional practice for such cases at that time. The child's father agreed and wished to follow doctors' orders. But the mother resisted. Against medical advice, she took her daughter home. She hired a speech pathologist to work on her daughter's language and a nanny who would encourage her daughter's social skills.

In time, the child not only spoke but engaged with others, though never in a completely effortless way. Her mother placed her in regular schools along with support. The girl proved to be extremely intelligent. Though she continued to struggle socially, she was remarkably successful academically. She earned a bachelor's degree in psychology, a master's degree in animal science, and a PhD in animal behavior.

That girl was Temple Grandin. A name you likely know. Today, she's a renowned animal behaviorist and advocate for the humane treatment of animals, and is an author, speaker, respected scientist, and a professor at Colorado State University. Formally diagnosed with autism, she is also a champion for the autism community and the neurodiversity movement.[5] Her efforts to give scientists and the world rare insight into what it is like to be on the autism spectrum have been invaluable. HBO even made a feature film of her life in 2010.[6]

What Temple Grandin has achieved in her lifetime is astonishing. But just as astonishing is that it all came to be because her mother, Eustacia Purves Cutler, trusted in her personal knowing and claimed it. Against all conventional wisdom, against all odds, breaking every model at the time, she "knew" what was necessary for her child to reach her full potential and brilliance, and she did it.

WHEN YOU KNOW, YOU KNOW

Knowing is not something you're gifted "at" or "with." The term "gifted" itself plays into The Model's hierarchy—putting one person or type of knowledge on a pedestal above another, which, as you now know, labels us and separates us. Knowing is not positive, prosperity, or law-of-attraction thinking. Knowing is not a mantra to repeat until you believe something. Those are nothing more than tricks of the mind that rob us of our energy and intention, and sometimes cause us to reject our original impressions and alter how we feel. To know is to acknowledge the positive and the negative—to acknowledge what is real, so you can trust in it and make powerful decisions about your

---

5   "Dr. Temple Grandin—Bio," The Association of People Supporting Employment First, 2022, https://www.apse.org/wp-content/uploads/docs/Temple%20Grandin's%20Bio.pdf; "Temple Grandin, 1947–," The Autism History Project, University of Oregon, https://blogs.uoregon .edu/autismhistoryproject/people/temple-grandin-1947.

6   *Temple Grandin*, written by Christopher Monger and William Merritt Johnson, directed by Mick Jackson, aired February 6, 2010, on HBO.

life from it. It is a guiding energy deep within us that is calm, easy, and certain—even when we aren't.

Happily, we don't have to go searching for our knowing. We don't even have to work to generate it consciously. It is already within us—a natural part of who we are. Every one of us is born knowing. We know our mother's voice. We know to eat. We know to cry to call attention to our needs. As newborns, our actions and reactions are immediate and correct. Our natural state is energized and effective, not anxious or depressed.

While our knowing never leaves us, as we grow older, The Model's pull can make our knowing less pronounced in our awareness, and therefore, more difficult to access. But it is always there. Even now, I'm betting you can feel your knowing within you. That sense that tugs at you with an undeniable sense of certainty well before the outcomes are evident. "I knew something was off." "I knew that would happen." "I knew I was in the right place." It's that thing you can't put your finger on, but you receive the message loud and clear—sometimes even enough to make you act. For instance, when you felt that nudge to drive home another way, only to find out later that the highway you didn't take was clogged due to an accident. Or you sensed something was off with your child, only to discover they had some difficult news. Or when you sensed someone was ill, though they said nothing and no symptoms were obvious, only to find out later what you sensed was true. This isn't magic. It is our most innately intelligent part offering us the easier way and prodding us to trust ourselves fully.

What I am describing here might feel like a different way of being to you and contrary to how you do things now. Yet, I suspect none of what I'm saying feels foreign. Since your knowing is within you always—and always has been—you feel it surface from time to time because it is natural to who you are. It is The Model that is imposed upon you. Bringing awareness to that fact alone will change how you see and do things, taking your life in a direction more suited to authentic you.

KNOWING DOESN'T ALWAYS MAKE SENSE

When our personal knowing agrees with our cultural model, we regard it as "common sense." And it is easy to claim and act on. But when our knowing contradicts The Model—as yours may be doing right now if you feel stuck or out of alignment—it can seem like it makes no sense, like it is a crazy thought or an impossibility. So it is hard to listen to and defend, let alone act on. Temple Grandin's father and her doctors might have considered her mother's decision to keep her daughter at home as foolish and not reality-based. Eustacia Purves Cutler might even have doubted herself. You likely have doubted what you know as well.

Strangely enough, my dislike of the phrase "everything is connected" showed me the way to trusting in my knowing. The phrase itself always felt off to me—so much so that I got perturbed when I heard someone say it. But when I took time out to think about the phrase, what arrived in my mind was a logic statement: "If everything is connected, there is nothing that cannot be connected." The second part of the statement clarified the first part for me—making it easy to accept its logic and truth. I also understood that this is how our knowing works: It asks us to believe in the first part (our sense), which is nonlinear, non–time-bound, and then it asks us to trust that the second part (the proof) will show up and make our knowing logical. In other words, our knowing asks us to trust before the proof is delivered. Being non–time-bound and nonlinear makes it a quantum feature. That's why our knowing can seem irrational. It only gives us the first part when it comes to us as a sense or thought. To get the second part—the proof—we have to act on that first part and see what plays out.

For instance, let's say the weather report says sun all day, but you sense you need to take an umbrella with you. That sounds irrational in the moment, right? Later your partner calls to tell you they have to work late and asks if you can pick up the kids at the soccer field. When you get there, the game is in overtime. As you stand on the sidelines in the blistering sun, that umbrella comes in handy to shade you. The seemingly irrational becomes rational.

Knowing rarely arrives with supporting facts. We have no idea how we came to this thought, idea, or feeling—what information and experiences formed it. It certainly doesn't offer us any guarantees as to outcomes if we do act on it. Like the elephants we discussed in Chapter 1, humans come to their knowing through sensing patterns and energy in our environment, and from other people. (HSPs are especially adept at this.) Using these patterns and energy, we know who we are and what's happening at a far deeper level than our rational mind—and for some, their conscious mind—allows. It is what's quantum about us. It is how the idea of taking an umbrella on a cloudless day comes to us. (We'll talk more about patterns in Chapter 7.)

When it comes to our knowing, we can't apply reason to calm our doubts and fears or help us justify going against The Model. We must simply trust in it—and believe ourselves—before the proof shows up. In the science-dependent world we live in, this is asking a lot. We've had years of conditioning in dismissing and devaluing what we feel, no matter how strongly we feel it. Negating all that and going with our personal knowing alone can seem as risky as it is unfamiliar. Just thinking about acting on our knowing can be overwhelming.

Personally, once aware of my knowing, instead of trusting in it, I challenged it—heeding the umbrella-type information only about 50 percent of the time. Even in challenging it, I could see what my knowing would have yielded had I followed it—as I was left with the natural consequences of discounting it. From there, it didn't take long for me to learn to trust in my knowing and in myself. Like all things in life, it was a process.

YOUR KNOWING IS YOU

Even if we choose to completely ignore our personal knowing, it doesn't go away. That nagging discomfort you feel as you do what is "expected" is your reminder that you're not doing what you were meant to do. That uncomfortable feeling that you "don't know who you are" motivates you to believe in where your knowing is calling you to go, who it is calling you to be. As an HSP, you feel that pull even deeper. It's up to you to pay attention to it or not, to accept it or not, to act on it or not—which is the challenge.

When you do choose to act on your knowing, you are by definition acting from your sweet spot—and you can feel it long before you see the results. Your personal knowing is where your innate talents lie, where your motivation lives, where what you dream for yourself becomes a choice you can make and live out. When you trust in your knowing and follow that wisdom—your wisdom—in time, your decisions and behaviors naturally align with the truth of who you are. When you live in that kind of alignment, everything eventually makes sense and falls into place. You are where you want to be, doing what you want to do, with everything you need.

Playing into The Model only steals your agency and limits your potential. Acting on what you know results in exactly the opposite. While our personal knowing does not always let us in on what is going to happen or how, it does prove over and over again that it is worth paying attention to and following. It makes us aware there is more than one path to success, more than one type of success to choose. It highlights what makes us different and unique from others. It allows us to expand our thinking within ourselves so we can show up as ourselves and impact the world in our own powerful way—more than The Model would ever allow. In the end, when we let it, our knowing reveals what is possible for us.

REVIVING OUR KNOWING

While your knowing is always there, it can take some practice to recognize and pay attention to it again after a lifetime of dismissing it. As you make the effort to bring it more fully into your awareness, you want to do so with curiosity and without judgment. (Negative self-judgment belongs to The Model.) Be gentle with yourself as well as playful with whatever arrives. Your knowing doesn't make you special. Everybody's got it. What you do with your knowing allows you to be uniquely yourself and confident in that.

As I worked on reconnecting with my personal knowing, I kept my life quiet and close until I felt more sure, more empowered. I found it helpful to step away from anyone (including family members) who made it too tempting for me to fall back into old patterns and The Model. I stayed away from anyone I knew would be forceful in telling me how I "should" behave or what I "should" do and anyone who felt compelled to express their concern about my choices or my future. You can identify such people in your own life by noticing how you feel after being with them. If you leave a meeting with them full of self-doubt and self-recrimination, that's your cue they are dragging you back into

The Model with them. You need space to be yourself, not suggestions on how to solve things in your life or take on another's judgment or criticism of you.

Perhaps this sounds a bit lonely. Most of us are hungry for connection, but taking a step back for you is only until you can hear yourself again. Once you can, you'll find yourself more open to being yourself and so attracting people who can honestly and deeply connect with you. My own journey to reconnection was decades of feeling like I couldn't take a breath. For all those years, however, my knowing held a reassurance inside me. I knew that one day I'd emerge from the life I was living inside The Model, and then I would have plenty of room in which I would be able to expand. I would not only have air to breathe, but I would be able to be me.

Reading energy—what I do—has never drained me. Why? Because I quickly learned how to be in my power with it. I knew it was what I was meant to do—even when I resisted and challenged it, which was a lot over my lifetime. I was not reverent with it. Yet somehow, I knew my intuition—my ability to read energy—of which personal knowing is one facet, was part of who I am and how I'm built. It allowed me to always feel some degree of connection regardless of how The Model made me feel disconnected from others. It allowed me to be confident in and allow for my fuller intuition without feeling like I needed to prove or promote my abilities or myself.

When you let your personal knowing guide you toward what is truly right for you—whatever that uniquely is for you—you too will feel the unmistakable energy and accompanying confidence to do it. For instance, maybe you have a boss whose behavior is so obnoxious that it forces you to reevaluate your work situation and ask yourself what you really want for yourself. Or maybe, like Eustacia Purves Cutler, you've received advice from an expert that doesn't sit well with you, and you feel compelled to do what you think is best instead. As you work to reveal your knowing, become more aware of what is happening in your life and which experiences may be invitations for you to employ what you know, and from that create change that moves you closer to where you are meant to be.

As a bonus, our example of living out our knowing gives others in our lives permission to do the same. After separating from my spouse and with both of my children in college, I decided to travel and then live abroad. I will talk more about how this choice helped me strengthen my connection to my knowing in upcoming chapters, but for now, the point is that some people judged me for this decision. But others told me my travels inspired them—giving them the confidence to follow their own hearts. This is the core of connection: You be you. I'll be me. And we will do it together, or we won't. Either way is okay.

Remember, your knowing is not an ultimatum. What feels right for you today is right for you today. Ten years from now, you may find yourself doing something completely different. When you change direction, put it in the proper perspective. It is not an indication that you once made a bad decision. It is a sign that you're ready for the next thing. Your aim is to return to your life, the one you truly came to live—where the inward you is fully reflected outward. Seeing past experiences as things to grow through instead of judging frees up room for us to make choices that expand our life.

ONLY YOU KNOW THE WAY

Once you can trust in your personal knowing and use it to guide your life, your life becomes uniquely and fully yours. Living outside The Model means living in your own power, where you see there is nothing to protect. The energy of others does not affect you because your knowing allows you to recognize those ruled by The Model. You now understand their aims, their fears, their manipulations, and that it is your choice whether you let them in your life or move away from them. It is your choice if you allow them to drain your energy by managing their constant aim to get you to stay in The Model so they can control you. You trust yourself in place of pleasing The Model because you know that when you move away, other, more powerful, more supportive people will arrive in your life.

Being free of The Model and trusting in your knowing bring about your literal best behavior—meaning behavior that leads to you honestly walking your own journey in life, the journey you were born to walk. You are not just doing things "your way." You are doing them in a way that stems from how you are uniquely built and results in living to your full and unique potential in this world. When you can feel and follow your knowing, you live out a powerful form of your natural order, which brings about a natural equality.

Living life is an art form, not a science. The Model prescribes a way to live that extinguishes that art and its beauty, along with the creative spirit each of us brings to the world. When we let people (including children) be themselves, they find their power and their way in life. But when we disturb them, give them too many rigid rules, and question their choices again and again, they lose their power and spend their lives in a struggle to reclaim it. The same goes for us. Each of us flourishes when we remove ourselves from an untrue life, releasing with it heavy loads of stress. You were not meant to endure your life; you were meant to live it.

If you have a good life, it can be hard to say something is wrong. It can feel like complaining. It can be even harder to trust in yourself that you know what is best for you. The message here is to keep going. Remember, only you know what you know. Only you can find out what that is. Only you can decide to claim it and act on it. Personal knowing is personal, after all.

As you move forward, remember that you can choose to trust in or challenge your knowing when it shows up. Either way, you'll learn and grow. Just don't dismiss it. As you discover more about it, expand on that. It is truly that simple. Gentle and steady; no need to push. You already know.

Chapter Five

TRUST: KNOWING'S ACTIVE INGREDIENT

W hen a baby feels hungry, they don't deny it. They cry out. When a young child senses unfairness during play, they don't let it be. They name the offense and the offender and demand that fairness be restored. As we have established, adult-you still feels your knowing and the urge to act on it. You know when you are hungry, when you are outraged, and when you are denying what's true. You have simply grown out of the habit of trusting in your knowing enough to act on it.

Think about a time when you were at a retreat, a yoga class, or even a business seminar—any environment where you and everyone else in the room had the space and permission to be safe and feel secure and free within yourselves, to look at your reality without judgment. I'm guessing that while you were there and for some time after, you felt pretty great. Maybe even a little high. That is because you clearly saw and could express who you are, what you wanted, and therefore for a moment, you knew the right way forward for you. You felt some possibility, maybe even some certainty. At that moment, you were experiencing the safe place of using vulnerability to nurture your creativity. You were in touch with some of your power. Yes, there would be hurdles—but you saw those clearly too and were motivated and determined to work through them to get to where you knew you were meant to be.

Once back in your everyday environment, however, you became weighed down by The Model—its expectations making you no longer feel you had the permission or the right to act on your knowing. The good feelings faded along with your clarity and creativity. Doubt crept into your psyche and your plans. You lost trust in your knowing and found yourself second-guessing and stuck once again.

This scenario is all too familiar for most of us. The good news here is that you've proved you can access your knowing and recognize it. Your challenge now is to go beyond that momentary recognition, to develop the needed trust and strengthen it so you can hold onto your knowing and act on it with conviction for the long haul. You want to be able to maintain your resolve not just in supportive environments but in tough, Model-laden ones too (also known as everyday life).

THE IMPORTANCE OF TRUSTING IN OURSELVES

Several years ago, I was listening to National Public Radio's *Invisibilia*—a show described as exploring "invisible forces that shape human nature." The episode I was listening to, "How to Become Batman," was about the idea that others' beliefs about and expectations for us affect our behavior and thus our potential.[7] Most of the episode centers on

---

7   Alix Spiegel and Lulu Miller, hosts, *Invisibilia,* podcast, season 1, episode 3, "How to Become Batman," National Public Radio, January 22, 2015, https://www.npr.org/programs/invisibilia/378577902/how-to-become-batman.

Daniel Kish, a man who suffered eye cancer as a baby, resulting in his total blindness. His mother, Pauline, explains that she saw her choice as "to wrap him in cotton" or let him be in the world like any other child.

When parents put The Model's expectations on our children, we are saying to them and ourselves that we know what is best for them. When we allow our fear to keep them from engaging the world the way they feel drawn to, what we are really doing is trampling on their knowing, making them doubt themselves, and making them dependent on us to know what to do and how they should be. Unwittingly, we are controlling either by being authoritarian or by enabling, just as we discussed in Chapter 2 and just like The Model wants us to. We are keeping them from growing and developing trust in themselves, in their knowing. What we parents often miss is our real responsibility to step back and give our children the opportunity to access and use their own knowing in their formative years, so they can live their lives as they are meant to.

Overriding fear, Kish's mother did take that step back and chose to trust her child to find his way. As a toddler, Kish seemingly instinctively started clicking his tongue. Those clicks bounced off whatever was in his surroundings, resulting in a "sonic representation" of his environment to him. What he was doing was "echolocating," a word that neither he nor his mom were familiar with. Bats navigate their world in much the same way—hence, the episode's title.

As he grew, Kish became so adept at echolocating that he eventually could safely walk to school by himself. He also climbed trees, found his way around new places, became an avid hiker, and even taught himself to ride a bike. Through echolocating, he said he can "see" his environment, just in a different way. During the program, he accurately described the landscape around him as he led the reporter on a hike through the woods. When researchers put him in an MRI and played a tape of his clicking sounds as he made his way in an environment, his brain's visual cortex lit up. Kish described his childhood and his adult life today as not much different from his sighted friends.

Interestingly in those early years, Kish's mother thought his clicking was something he alone did, a coping mechanism he made up, but the clicking is not unique to him. The episode reports that left to do what comes naturally to them (i.e., follow their knowing), most blind children begin clicking to echolocate as intuitively as they begin talking, walking, or accomplishing any other developmental task—which of course increases their independence, opening the world and all its opportunities to them. Sadly, unlike Kish, most blind children are discouraged from developing this skill. Parents and society at large typically put a stop to it—not understanding what it's about and believing the noise of it to be socially unacceptable (in other words, outside The Model). When Kish's regular public school complained that his clicking was disruptive to others in his class, his mother told them it was necessary for him and would have to be accommodated.

According to *Invisibilia*, when Kish was about ten years old, he met a boy named Adam, who was about the same age and was educated at a school for the blind. Adam's inability to do things for himself frustrated Kish. Kish responded by rejecting Adam and was unkind to him. However, the thought of Adam never left Kish. It haunted him into adulthood. While sorry that he hadn't been nicer to the child, Kish also couldn't help but think how different Adam's life could have been if he had been able to develop his natural echolocation skills.

Though Kish said he never imagined or consciously wanted his career to have anything to do with blindness, he found himself drawn toward a need to educate the world to recognize echolocation as another type of vision and to teach the skill to those who wanted to learn. I imagine Kish knew echolocation had the power to change lives; that he knew that most blind people could live as fully as he did if given the chance to develop this innate skill. Trusting in that knowing and acting on it—a capacity he'd been developing all his life—Kish founded World Access for the Blind, a foundation whose tagline is "Our vision is sound."[8] Beyond advocating for and teaching echolocation, the organization strives to get the public to see that those with vision impairment or blindness are more than capable of living life as they wish, under their own direction, doing what they want to do.

Invisibilia used the episode to delve into how others' respective expectancies and expectations determine our behavior and what becomes possible for us—for better or worse. I took away from the show that where we are allowed, loved, and even encouraged to be ourselves and follow our knowing, we set our own expectations for ourselves, which obviously shapes what we do in our lives. Kish's mom acted outside The Model, trusting in her son. His mom's belief encouraged his own nature, and he expressed and expanded himself without the burden of The Model. Because of The Model–free environment his mother created, Kish was free to trust in what he did know as a child, and through natural consequences, he learned the rest. The only thing standing in our way of being who we are meant to be is taking the initiative to follow our knowing, making the first move, and learning from there. Kish's life exemplifies what is possible when we stay true to who we are and what we know, and grow through the natural consequences that result.

FEAR AND WORRY

That is not to say trusting in our knowing isn't easier said than done. It demands that we overcome big hurdles in our mind—the most

---

8   World Access for the Blind, https://waftb.net.

common being fear and worry. Most of us get stopped by one little phrase: "But what would happen if . . ." But what would happen if I quit my steady job to run my own business? If I said I didn't want to do the bake sale this year? If I didn't nag my kids to get to bed on time? Past traumas are triggered, highly charged emotions ensue. Typically, we don't even bother to answer the question. The fear shuts us down before we take a chance.

The fear may cause us to worry. Even "knowing" that worry is useless—that it is nothing more than an invitation to spend energy in a futile pursuit to control what cannot be controlled (the future)—does not stop the worry. Before we have even tried, fear and worry send the message: "I don't think I can," or "I don't think you can," or "I don't think we should." Worry prompts us to project our fears onto a situation and onto others—causing drama and leading to guilt and withholding information that might clarify a situation for all. The drama so many people are fond of creating only serves to make issues seem bigger than they are, avoiding facts and disallowing the possibility of tangible solutions.

Both Kish and his mother faced scary moments. Kish made errors in judgment—errors he may not have made had he been typically sighted. And he suffered some natural consequences that were hard on him and for his mom looking on, such as losing teeth in bike riding accidents more than once. But as his mother reasoned, accidents happened to every kid growing up. Better to suffer a few setbacks as a child and learn from them than to never do the things that call to you in life.

Because the challenges most of us face aren't as stark or immediate as the Kish family's, we can more easily reason our way out of committing to stand firm against The Model whenever we feel worried, anxious, or uncomfortable—whether about our kids or ourselves. After all, worry and fear are appropriate at times. For instance, if a doctor said you likely have cancer but you were still awaiting the test results, it is reasonable to worry and feel a range of emotions. But when we are deciding to follow our knowing, to risk going outside The Model, to take action necessary to live how we feel called to live, then we serve our life best by choosing what we know and allowing others—even our children—to choose for themselves.

Though The Model tells us it is part of parenting to worry about our children, when you drill down, much of that worry stems from our attachment to their achieving what we believe are the right outcomes for them—instead of trusting in their knowing what is best. Like any attachment, this one results in anxiety that we then try to soothe by retreating to The Model, leading to more anxiety.

My journey to no longer second-guessing my actions and being honest no matter who I was engaging with took twenty-two years and continues to evolve. Don't worry; I am sure you will get there much faster than I did. As you work toward increasing your trust in your knowing, expect the process to feel challenging, abstract, lonely, and at points, weird. You might find yourself on a plateau now and then, knowing the direction you are meant to go but unable to push the boundaries of The Model further. You might rest there awhile. But once you start down this road (and by the way, reading this book says you've already started), you won't be able to turn back. This alone affirms you came born for the future.

Relearning trust in myself and gaining the confidence to stand with my knowing took practice, and guts—especially when it came to parenting. For instance, I remember once when my children were home from college on winter holiday, a neighbor invited us all to a birthday party. Her adult kids were also home from school, and she thought our children would enjoy this opportunity to be together. In truth, I thought that too. But my children declined the invitation. They had already made other plans for that evening. When I called my neighbor to tell her it would only be me attending, she tried to lay a guilt trip on me—telling me I "should" insist my children attend, trying to pull me into The Model's way of how things "should" be done.

I did not join her in The Model—nor in the guilt and shame that were waiting there for me. I did not worry that my actions might cause a rift between us or that she might ostracize me from the neighborhood community. I trusted in my knowing, which told me to trust my adult children to make decisions for themselves. My knowing kept me clear and acting on my conviction that my children's choices were theirs to make, not mine.

Once you are aware of and feel your knowing, you can start to relate to it. And when you get to that place where you trust your knowing freely, nothing can stand in your way—and nothing feels better than that. You come alive because you are with your own form of expression, you are connected. This is the point where abundance meets you in kind, opening the doors you need to pass through to get to where you were meant to be. However even then, it is still up to you to trust your knowing enough to walk through them.

NATURAL CONSEQUENCES

When we do have the nerve to follow our fear-based questions to their logical conclusion, we find out the only thing that "happens if" you take the action on your knowing are natural consequences. For instance, if you quit your job to own your own business, you might find great financial reward. But you might also find struggle. You might even fail—which could set you back financially until you figure out your next move. Or you might be no better off financially, find you work a lot more, but that you are more fulfilled as a person and enjoy being an entrepreneur. Or if you are totally blind and use echo-location to learn to ride a bike, you might give yourself a whole new mode of getting around town. Or if you start shouting "Look at me!" instead of clicking to monitor the environment you're in, you might run into a building and lose some teeth. All are possibilities. All have natural consequences when not acting in your knowing. However, the more you are honest and push into what isn't working, the more you will indeed find the right people, places, and situations that see you through in greater and greater ways and into situations you could never have dreamed of.

If you are prepared to accept those consequences, then you can put your fear—and all its accompanying woes—aside. You can see the situation through a clear enough lens and from a neutral place. You can trust that the natural consequences are the right consequences for you. You can trust that even the seemingly bad ones will work to reconnect you to something greater: to your own power. In time and with experience, you find you stop asking, "But what would happen if." You stop being afraid of the consequences because you trust them to put you in proper alignment with your life and what you value.

Keep in mind, not acting on your knowing has natural consequences too—consequences you might be living out right now. In my younger days, I would have been so apprehensive about telling my neighbor that my children declined her invitation that I would have pushed my knowing aside and allowed my fear to guide me. As a result, I would have worried about her judgment of me for days, tried to cajole my children into doing something other people (not even me, really) wanted them to do, and then I would have felt like both a bad mother and a bad neighbor. On top of all that, I would have delayed speaking to my neighbor and not accepted or declined her invitation in a timely manner—making me legitimately rude, giving her a real reason to judge me, and giving me one more thing to feel bad about. Also worth noting, my withholding information from my neighbor would have landed me on the abusive side of The Model. In enabling this situation for my neighbor—controlling her with misinformation—I would be denying her an honest response, leaving her to draw and act on incorrect conclusions in the future. In the end, those natural consequences of following The Model instead of trusting in my knowing would have taken great energy from me, all while making me miserable and serving no positive purpose.

In contrast, the natural consequences of my trusting in my knowing and acting on it included my neighbor being a little peeved and arguing with me (though that was probably going to happen no matter how I did it). I was, after all, stepping away from The Model—and that's often uncomfortable for people we are interacting with. However, on the positive side, our interaction was an honest one. She encountered the real me. Whether or not she liked that was up to her, not me. Standing in my knowing also let me see that her anger had nothing to do with me and more to do with her expectations for fulfilling The Model. Her motivation—whether or not she knew it—was to transfer her insecurities to me, making us both more stressed. Most everyone who clings to The Model wants to play hot potato with their emotions, hoping for some reprieve from carrying their energy-draining feelings themselves.

To me, the most important natural consequence of trusting in my knowing was that once again my children witnessed me believing in their decision-making capabilities and standing by them. They trusted me more because they knew I trusted them. Not only did this cause our relationship to strengthen once again, but it was another opportunity for them to build their trust in themselves as they made their way to independence and maturity. My expansion made room for my children's expansion.

Nothing can touch or bother you when you let your knowing guide you. You are always in the right place for you. Outside The Model, it is not in our nature to worry, feel guilty, cause drama, or withhold information. What is natural is to trust ourselves and our circumstances as they are. This is what removes the hierarchy and its judgments from our personal experience. This is what lifts resistance and creates freedom in our lives. This is what gives us the confidence to make our own choices and manage our own lives. If we each know our power, show it, and share it with one another, undeniably everything changes for the better. Each of us shines in our own way.

THE WHEAT FROM THE CHAFF

When we are able to trust in our knowing and act on it, we let go of what makes us play small—our anger, disillusion, insecurity, worry, and fear. We give room to what inspires and motivates us, and to our own evolution. Our trust gives us the confidence to act, restoring the natural order and ensuring abundance in our lives and in the world.

This is not to say you don't research and listen to advice before making big decisions. It is to say that when you feel you have all the information you need, you check in with yourself and allow the final decision to be yours, to come from your personal knowing. If you do not know, then until you do know, the answer is "no." When the nudge feels like "yes," but the answer is murky, push into the action in a small way to test the water. For example, if you are starting a business, call contacts who can help. Or if you are a stay-at-home parent who is thinking about returning to work, call other parents who have been in your shoes. Through actions like these, you start to create a network of information. By getting the facts you mitigate drama. You also neutralize your fear. By filling in the pieces, you step forward more confidently and see where it leads you. Give it space. Let it happen.

Choosing our knowing always moves us toward fulfillment, even if sometimes the road is rocky getting there. Challenges and momentary discomforts—like admitting that some relationships or goals we have pursued need to be rethought and maybe let go—are to be expected. However, if you find yourself second-guessing your decision after you have committed to it, you owe it to yourself to take a moment and ask if perhaps The Model might be trying to pull you back in.

After my husband and I told everyone in our lives that we were divorcing, I had the opportunity to visit Ireland for a few weeks. Since I was seriously considering living abroad, I thought it might do me good, so I took off. At the end of my visit, sitting in the Dublin airport waiting for my flight home, I asked myself if I was ready to go back to the US or if I wanted to stay in Ireland longer. I've known since I was in my twenties that Europe was the place for me. And my knowing was making it clearer and clearer to me each day that my heart needed a home. As I thought through my questions, I felt neutral—meaning I didn't care if I went home or stayed in Ireland. While I'd felt neutral at other times in my life, this was different. I had never felt quite this way before.

Upon returning to the United States, I heard passively through two sources that when you are this type of neutral, it means your trauma is not informed. I was fully with myself: Nothing needed forcing. Nothing needed doing. This notion sat right with me.

Over the next two years, I'd find myself not only returning to Ireland several times but living all over the world. My travels helped me grow out of my fears. Traveling also helped me shed bits of The Model in areas of my life where those natural consequences had been blocked, due to my living a seemingly certain yet unfulfilling life. I slowly unfurled from feeling stuck, low, confused, and anxious—a reflection not of who I am but a sign of the breakdown of who I'm not.

Simultaneously, I was still in the process of severing my marriage partnership. I knew it was time. I also knew that it had been an important partnership that had served us both, but that now blocked us both from fully expressing who we truly are. It had accomplished all it could, and moving on was the right course. Trusting in that knowing made me calm, kept me clear, and gave me strength through knowing I was waiting for me on the other side of this experience.

I was sure. I only questioned my choice when I felt low about myself. This reinforced how low I'd felt inside of the marriage, trying to be me and never succeeding. Then, I noticed something else totally surprising: I was sleeping at night. I felt like me. For the first time in my adult life, I felt myself showing up as me. Not someone trying to override my own feelings to meet an expectation. Not someone playing to The Model. Not someone hiding from everyone, including myself. I was me, powerfully me.

Trusting in our knowing moves everything out of our way that doesn't serve us. Our job is to make the change needed. Stepping out of The Model is a must. Those consequences you keep experiencing are telling you to make a change. They are your signal to return to you. As we watch things play out, we start to understand the full picture of why things happen the way they do in our lives—whether it is a flight getting canceled, a car breaking down, or winning the lottery. When we are able to trust in the pattern as it is happening, we can relax and let life unfold, giving up control even while signing divorce papers.

Today, I mostly make my home in Europe. If you would have told me ten years ago that this would be my life, I would not have believed you. Yet, I would also have to admit that when I was a child, I knew I needed a life that afforded expansion. I always wanted more. And I was always told I wanted too much. I acquiesced to The Model for decades. I became afraid to want or be too much. I didn't even consider going to college out of state—compromising my life and potential. But by returning to trusting in my knowing, to trusting in myself, I have built the confidence to live to my full potential. Trust has brought me a long way. I guarantee it will do the same for you.

TRUST YOUR PROCESS

As we have discussed, the way out of The Model is to ask yourself the basics of what you want; start small and your knowing can show up and move you to what is next. This way, you learn to trust and follow that knowing—which takes self-confidence, determination, and commitment. It takes doing it repeatedly because knowing operates from patterns. We hold the vision for ourselves; our actions are our vote for how we shape our future. Acting in The Model will not achieve what we collectively desire. When we guide ourselves, trust in our knowing, and let go, our life patterns become more and more clear. Trusting ourselves gives us power. It is only logical that when we allow our uniqueness to shine by putting ourselves in appropriate situations where we thrive and with people who champion it, the need to control or enable falls away, and trust takes its place.

The more you exercise your self-awareness and self-expression, the more efficient and comfortable you become at feeling what you know and trusting it. Trusting in our knowing builds on itself in a perfect way for each person. In time, perhaps you will operate purely from knowing and hone this part of you fully. I want you to be the next person who creates something truly new on earth because it was your birthright to do so, and you listened to yourself instead of playing small. Trust is your pathway there. Those who trust in their knowing and do what makes their life sing create a path for others to do the same. Those who are doing the opposite create a stifling Model-based life filled with meaningless hierarchy, purpose-lessness, and lost potential, chasing expectations in place of passion. The choice is yours. It is always yours.

As you reacquaint yourself with your knowing, do things that make you feel powerful. Avoid anything (or person) that feels like a rut. Even some activities and practices that are supposed to boost self-awareness can still perpetuate The Model if you force them on yourself or cling to them to prove you are a certain way (we'll talk more about this in Chapter 7). But mostly keep in mind that this is a process. And a slow one at that. Reconnecting to your knowing can be a back-and-forth. A trusting and not trusting. A connecting and then pulling back when fear reenters your mind and trauma may signal attention to be resolved. Like life, it comes through trial and error. It comes through changing patterns. And like life, mistakes will be made. Sometimes you may even feel stuck again. When you experience a perceived failure, remember that a natural consequence will move you back onto your path.

Part of the process is accepting you are in a process. It takes rep-etition to clinch the understanding necessary for deeply trusting what you know. Once you start, the changes will lead you to your full expression and your future. You will trust more deeply in spaces of your life where you were not able to trust before. Only then do synchronicities come to light. Only then do you shed emotions you didn't know you were harboring. Energy drains, like second-guessing yourself and other people's judgment, fall away. You put yourself first without feeling selfish because, in truth, you are not being selfish—knowing is altruistic, and therefore, the best for everyone, even if those in The Model cannot understand that in the moment. You no longer dismiss yourself or compromise who you are. You come into your power. Life begins to make sense again. With every step, you make your way—in your own way.

Chapter Six

RESISTANCE-FREE LIVING

Several years ago, I experienced regular bouts of physical symptoms that made me feel like I was dying. Doctor after doctor couldn't diagnose me. When I questioned the wide-ranging results of my tests—especially my varying blood markers—I was met with "That means nothing." Some of the doctors told me to wait it out, that my cycles of pain would probably go away. Others advised me to learn to live with it. Some told me my pain was "in my head."

Now I understand these doctors—like many professionals—were steeped in The Model. They were not accepting and letting go to their own knowing—knowing that would allow them to acknowledge that they did not know. If they had been attuned to their knowing, they would have been able to accept what I was reporting and be curious about it. They'd have been able to use their creativity and experience, along with their medical knowledge to overcome any resistance The Model presented to them and solve the challenge before them. They would have been unafraid to say, "I don't know what is behind your pain, but let's work together to find out." All of us want a doctor like that.

The Model supports hierarchy in place of collaboration, however. It tells us to look to the doctor, to trust in the doctor, and that the doctor knows more than we do about our own health. But since the doctor wasn't helping in this case, I had to choose to trust in my knowing. Honestly, when it came to my medical care, I didn't want to step away from the system. I'm no expert in that arena. A family member even told me I would ruin my health by doing so—which concerned me.

But desperation and pain often drive us to listen to that voice inside us. Ironically, I got a push toward my knowing from a doctor. He told me he didn't know what was wrong with me, but he was sure something was wrong. And he caringly said, "If you were my wife or daughter, I would tell you to keep after this fiercely. Don't stop until you get answers." I used his kindness and concern to give me strength to fully accept what I knew—that something was causing my fatigue, pain, and more—something that could be discovered, diagnosed, and treated. I had no choice but to continue to search for answers. But now, I also had the added support of this doctor's belief in and caring for me, which gave me even more confidence to connect with my knowing in this process. And that is exactly what I did. Finally, after three years of searching, I found a physician who went beyond the usual protocol and used their creativity to reach the right diagnosis. Using the same tests and test results as the other doctors, this physician was able to determine that I had chronic Lyme disease. Deeper testing revealed I was riddled with the illness. It was no wonder I felt like I was dying.

When the system troubles you, it is often a catalyst for you to find your way to what is a match for you. It is a "natural consequence," bringing you to exactly where you need to be. As a consequence of this experience, I now see my health, doctors, and medicine in general as things I have a right to question. Today, I have an extremely financially accessible private physician who trusts me to know myself and welcomes my questions—which has helped me to become healthier than I would've ever been being treated within The Model. While finding my way here was hard won, it was, in the end, worth the realization that I have choices and know natural consequences lead me to something that is an exact match to who I am.

In the same vein, I trusted in a nudge telling me to write this book. I sat down and wrote more than two hundred pages over five years. As I read over the work as a whole, however, I got the sense I needed help from a professional to make the content flow better. So, I took a step into my vulnerability and asked a successful author I admire how she produced her book. As I write this, I am well into working with her editor, and the manuscript I intended is becoming a reality. (In fact, it now has become a published reality, and you are reading it!)

While the situations in these examples are very different, both illustrate how trusting in our knowing leads to no longer resisting reality—pleasant or not. Once there, points of resistance (like physicians who won't go the distance or no experience writing a book) become points of opportunity. We see what isn't working for us and know we can find a way that will.

Eventually, through our choices, the broken system falls away from our lives completely. That's because our choices now are guided by and focus on who we are, not on a broken system. And the natural consequence of those choices allows us to recognize what is true for us and our needs. We can see the incentives for moving toward a better way for us. Though it doesn't always feel great during the initial "breakdown" (i.e., doctors telling me my pain is in my head, two hundred pages that aren't quite right), the more we trust in the process, the easier it is to go with what we know. We step beyond The Model's limitations, live from our being, and see that our capability is far beyond the physical.

We even receive small confirmations along the way. I got one of those small confirmations when I started working with my editor on this book. Her name is Beth. The same week I started working with her, three other people named Beth came into my life. The unusualness of all those Beths coming into my life at the same time caught my attention, and, I felt, underscored that I was on the right track. During my first phone call with Beth my editor, we got a little off-subject and talked about names. She asked me if I knew what "Beth" meant. I said, "No." She told me it meant "home." I felt that. When you trust your knowing, the little signs that give you reassurance you're on the right path are there. When you allow for life's flow, you gain energy and momentum from it.

THE ADVANTAGE IN YOUR POWER

When we resist what we know, we operate from The Model's delusion and need to control us. We live and act according to what isn't, which is not only delusional but unproductive. We're left to make up stories instead of asking questions. We expend energy and emotion without getting what we really desire. Our lives become frustrating because our actions are self-defeating, as our maintaining "being good" gets us nowhere.

Had I allowed myself to depend on the system with both my illness and writing this book, the system would have controlled what was possible for me. I'd likely still be dealing with debilitating pain, not knowing the cause, and have a lot of pages written but no real book. In both cases, giving power to my own voice—my knowing—oriented me toward positive actions. I was able to see and do what needed to be done to get to where I was meant to go in my life.

Being in a constant fight with reality takes energy from your life. When you deny reality (which The Model often asks you to do), your resistance blocks life's flow, and you stay stuck. Often and not surprisingly, this leads to anger and then depression. On the other hand, when you trust in your knowing, you see and place your energy into the reality of the situation. Which means you invest your energy in meaningful ways. Coming from your power ensures your actions are based on the truth of what is, which is always more constructive and potent for your life than acting on a delusion of what "should" be.

When we are where we're meant to be—when we go where our knowing places us—things flow easily. For instance, when my son learned he would need more funding for college tuition based on the major he declared, he applied for several scholarships from a variety of sources. The three scholarships he won were all for further study in that major—and they more than covered his need. One was offered by his employer, a tutoring service in that field. It was for more money than he would have earned working for them over a semester. These were all signs that when he chose his major, he was in or very close to his personal knowing.

Not long after that, however, he told me he was thinking about changing his major. As he was uttering those words, something felt amiss to me. Initially, I felt concerned he was doubting himself, maybe a little overwhelmed by his success and how real it was becoming. I wondered if this uneasiness was causing him to retreat toward The Model. I took my unrest as a sign for me to step back, address my feelings behind the scenes, and come to him later.

The next time I saw him, I asked, "Are you changing your major because you are concerned about costs and maybe graduating with debt?" "No," he said. A few days later, I mentioned that he had seemed so excited about school in the previous semester and now he seemed less so. I asked if anything had changed. We both paused. He then opened up and told me he was feeling a little lost.

When we operate outside The Model, we can feel the pulse of others' emotions in a powerful way that helps create positive change. When we first sort out our side of the equation, we are then free of judgment and ready to ask the questions that bring clarity to the situation. This movement shifted me out of concern and back into a position of trust. It moved me back into my belief in my son, which serves him far more powerfully than my worry or concern. If he can articulate where he is, I know he'll experience natural consequences that will move him back to his knowing and back on his rightful path. All of which is his to decide, of course. Still, behind the scenes, I can be that powerful force of trust for my son because I know he knows. If he changes his major a million times, that's okay. It's not about that. It's about him staying true to himself and following that. Ensuring that his parent sees and hears him is my true job as a parent.

The power of our personal knowing is kryptonite to The Model. It upends the resistance created by fear and self-doubt. It positions you to take full advantage of life's flow. It changes your life for the better in myriad ways. Your personal knowing shows you there is another way and gives you the power to flow to it.

LETTING GO

Restoring your knowing and using your power, however, requires letting go. We must let go of the facade of and desire for the control The Model creates—as tempting as it is. We must believe—until we can see for ourselves—in a reality where we belong and don't control. This is where a lot of us get tripped up. The Model teaches us that "letting go" equates to powerlessness. In truth, it is exactly the opposite. Letting go is a powerful move—even a loving act.

What we have defined as power in our world is actually control, which must be fought for, maintained through authoritarian actions or enabling, and can be lost at any time. When you instead let go to what you know is true, you move through life without the false interferences of The Model. You develop a neutral response—meaning trauma, hierarchy, and status no longer inform your choices. Emotional triggers are replaced by understanding your life patterns, relinquishing their control over your thinking. Shoulds no longer prevent you from acting. Guided only by the clarity of what is, you approach situations from the vantage of possibility. You can see the right way forward for you and feel free to take it. Letting go to personal knowing frees you from illusions and cultural restraints. Living without extremes (right/wrong, good/bad) allows for a more nuanced and gentler day-to-day existence. When the shadow is healed, our clarity and uniqueness are revealed.

The power of your personal knowing combined with an ability to let go allows you to keep questioning but no longer doubting or second-guessing. Even when confronted with your deepest fears, you are at peace because you are no longer trying to fit into another's mold for you. Your knowing provides you with a clear sense of self and trust in your ability to guide your own life. Eventually, you live in full expression of who you are. Ultimately, you shine without device.

In my own life, I benefited from letting go when my marriage was over. I found my fear replaced with more true potential and my power. The state of mind the action of letting go afforded me allowed me to approach the details of our divorce in as healthy a way as possible for my former spouse and me, as well as for our children. By fully embracing that our relationship had run its course and allowing that to be, I didn't enter the negotiations emotionally charged or laden with old vendettas.

The proof is that my purpose and energy were clear. I was able to be respectful toward all that my former spouse and I had been through and accomplished together while realistic that it was time to undo the day in, day out partnership. While I was sad at times during the process, I wasn't angry. I was confident in the decision I made. I was sure that in the end, our divorce would leave everyone in a better place, even when it didn't feel great in the moment. (By the way, when you do decide to make substantive changes in your life—to leave a relationship or a job or whatever—consider working toward a balance between making plans, getting the facts, and allowing things just to happen.)

When I filed the papers to get divorced, I felt that same neutral state (free of trauma) that I felt waiting for my flight in Dublin. In that state, I was able to regard that final gesture more as an act of love, not malice—the moment felt pure and true. It was a sign of freedom from who I was not. Letting go to my knowing and acting out of that peace and certainty for my family made what could have been a turbulent time for all of us a time of individual growth for each of us. All of this was reflected to me when one of my children shared their thoughts on why their dad and I got divorced. They said, "So you could each be fully who you are." That is what life is about, after all. Our personal knowing champions this ability naturally.

Over time, our trust in our knowing continues to strengthen our power, which allows us to negate obstacles like the negative judgments of others, and leaves control behind. As our intentions and actions align, the people in our lives may cease their negativity about our choices and stop confronting us with their opinions. If they don't, your next step is to make a choice about boundaries.

RESISTANCE-FREE DOESN'T MEAN TROUBLE-FREE

While letting go and knowing do bring you to a place of neutrality and certainty in your direction, they don't guarantee an easy road ahead. As we have seen, trusting in your knowing and allowing it to guide you invites natural consequences, which are often difficulties. Some come with pain. Things we don't like happen—accidents, loss, illness, economic troubles, relationship issues. In dealing with these difficulties, The Model (which encourages us to please others or do what we are told because we feel unsure about what to do) can only ever lead us away from who we are. By choosing to trust in our true circumstances and the consequences of that—overriding The Model's influence to get us to second-guess ourselves—we are able to piece together the patterns that created where we are now. With that, we find our power and recognize the next step on our true path.

This, in turn, helps us deal with whatever resistance comes our way. And so, we become free of it. In my own life, many fears and unpleasant feelings surfaced as I worked through the challenges of parenting, my divorce, and my Lyme disease symptoms. When fears and uneasy feelings arose, my knowing allowed me to accept them as mine to manage. I could see they were opportunities to deeply process so I could move beyond them and gain more true power. As I wrote this book, fear would creep in from time to time—and the writing offered space for me to address that pain and the shadow parts within. The more I worked through those rough places, the happier and calmer I became, which I know sounds obvious because it is.

When we regard difficulties as a sign, we can disengage from what keeps us stuck and clear the way for something better for us. When we are able to let go of our need for control, we leave The Model, find peace, and ultimately, our greater expression. When you know where you are and find power in the natural consequence of it, you'll find you are supported—even if it doesn't feel that way at first. Our job is to recognize and handle what keeps creating pain or strife in our lives. As we do that, synchronicity takes hold. Remember, it is not up to you to see the destination. You only need to see the immediate step in front of you. Ultimately, finding your power creates order. If you can see your destination but not the steps, act on one thing, one fact, looking inside for your guidance. In contrast, worry and the need to control force us into another's way of being, which blocks us from the road to our knowing and living to our full potential.

Preparing for a journey from Spain to New Zealand, I felt some resistance to the trip as I purchased my plane ticket. Though I'm not normally afraid to fly, I was concerned about the flights from Madrid to Auckland. Something in me was being triggered. I didn't know what. I did know, though, that the fear was irrational, signaling to me that it came from a pattern inside me I could not see. I decided to trust unquestioningly, and I bought the plane ticket anyway.

On the first leg of my twenty-three hours of flying, the plane landed forty-five minutes late. As we taxied into the terminal, I worried out loud about making my connection. My seatmate heard me. It turned out she was traveling with a large group of educators from Denmark, who took up nearly every seat around me on the plane. They spread the word about my predicament. When the plane door opened, they all stayed in their seats, allowing me to get off the plane quickly. Thanks to their concern and generosity, I made my next flight in plenty of time. I was amazed and so thankful.

Just before I boarded the next plane for a twelve-hour flight, I was asked if I would give up my seat so a family could sit together. In trade, I would get an entire row to myself further back in the airplane. Of course, I said yes—and felt lucky to enjoy so much space on such a long flight.

Then on my last flight—lasting nine hours—I took my assigned seat by the window and watched as what I judged to be interesting people filled up my row. As we took off, the woman in the middle seat began to cry—she'd had a day filled with travel setbacks. The man sitting on the other side of her and I consoled her. Through this act of compassion, we discovered that the three of us had a lot in common. Though we were different ages, from different places, and had different life experiences, we found real connection with each other. That dreaded nine-hour flight was over in what seemed like no time. We talked and laughed the entire way.

Despite the fear I had felt about taking this journey, I arrived in Auckland feeling better and more self-assured than I had in some time. A few days later, it struck me why. My journey had been a microcosm of a world where people support and connect with each other. That's the kind of world I strive to create. The kind of world I want to be part of. The kind of world this trip allowed me to experience.

Note that I spent time and put my attention on my initial discomfort about taking this journey. Because I acknowledged and accepted my discomfort, I was able to address it, not override it, and so eventually, let it go. By the time I left for the airport, I felt much calmer. I was ready and curious to see what unfolded on this trip and was open to natural consequences. It was in the traveling portions of this trip—not in arriving at my destination—where I filled in the parts and pieces I needed to get back to my knowing. It was the resistance I addressed along the way and overcame by trusting in my own power and community that helped me reconnect fully to myself. As I made choices to step away from what was not working in my life and reached out to the unknown, my life got better, and my power increased.

LIVING IN THE REAL WORLD

Your life and what you do with it are unique to you. In some ways, the energy has not been on our side to make the shifts and changes we can now. Your knowing supports your uniqueness—even if where it is nudging you is uncomfortable or seems irrational in the moment.

When you proceed from your knowing, you proceed from a place of legitimacy. You drop the pretense. You stop rerunning patterns in your head and stop daydreaming and obsessing about what-ifs that can't be. Free of The Model's false fears and energy drains, you have more energy to act—and more personal power when you do act. You advance in your life because you live resistance-free. Confidently on the path to your own self-expression and way of being, you know the challenges you do face are there to help you develop, to push you further down the path to realizing what you can do, what you exclusively bring to the world for others, what you are truly capable of, and who you really are—all moving you closer to experiencing your full potential. That is what we all deserve and what brings us into a true sense of ourselves.

Negating or denying who we are and what we know—giving our power to The Model—limits our expression and so limits us. Feeling the need to fit in, to be right, to prove yourself, or to get in the last word are all signs you are not being honest and are not able to see who you really indeed are—which is something other than what people tell you.

As I mentioned in the introduction to this book, we are coming out of what I think are the highest universal levels of narcissistic expression that have ever been. There is a need to address the pain and trauma that has come with this experience. As you do, keep in mind that you are not that pain and that your trauma is not your fault. To engage your personal knowing, you must look inside at everything with self-awareness and challenge what you see. You must continually ask yourself if the life you are living is your choice or if The Model is making your choices for you.

As we become more self-aware, we can take matters into our own hands. For instance, we can be different parents than our parents were, giving our kids the example of how to live in personal knowing. We can address our feelings and move through them. We can work behind the scenes to recapture our true essence and see ourselves most fully. Through these actions, letting go and trusting in our power become natural. We free ourselves from ego when we free our personal knowing into its full expression. This supports us in identifying and finding the people and places that exalt our natural abilities.

Section Three

LIVING IN
THE KNOW

Chapter Seven

YOU ARE YOUR TEACHER

I once knew a woman who rejected everything she ever created—including her own children. It wasn't a reflection on the children, though it felt like that to them. What she was rejecting was any notion of her own value. After all, acceptance of who you are and what you bring forth in life is a vulnerable position. It can also be a joyful and resistance-free one. It calls you to say "yes" and stand up for yourself in countless ways—in what you believe, what you know, what you choose, and what you do.

But this woman—like all who cling to The Model—was afraid to be so vulnerable. She refused to look too deeply at anything or anyone, including herself. She didn't acknowledge disappointments and traumas, and she certainly didn't want to face the reality of them in her own life. She didn't want to see what they had to reveal to her about the world and maybe herself—and through that, perhaps find truth and healing. Instead, she stuck to the dictum that suffering is "something you just don't talk about." As The Model preaches, she stuffed her pain and soldiered on.

Anyone near her could almost see her struggling to hold her pain in—as if she were under constant threat of losing her mind if she released it. On occasion when the pressure proved too much, she would have small outbursts and childlike fits. While she both needed and deserved to throw those fits, her anger was usually misplaced toward her husband, her children, or both. In her mind, she told herself that someone had done something in the moment that annoyed her and caused her anger. I think deep inside she knew that anger was a constant presence in her life, made of a thousand unprocessed harms, and always brewing just beneath her skin. But that is something we will never know because she never stayed with any feeling long enough to get to the source of it, to take charge of her pain, and to take charge of herself.

I see this as a great loss for the world. Because even under those burdens of unprocessed trauma, denial, and the anger they produced, her intelligence and talents shone through. The power of her life force could not be denied.

This tragedy for this woman became a tragedy for her children. Though her children knew their mom had had challenges in her childhood, they never knew how exactly she came to be who she was. Being that they were children, their mother's anger wasn't theirs to attend to. But that is not to say it didn't affect them. It did, and greatly. In a case like this, children more often think everything is their fault. These children were no different. They not only thought their mother's rage was aimed at them but also caused by them. Some went so far as to reason that maybe if they didn't exist, then neither would their mother's anger. Living and maturing under constant threat creates children who feel uncertain and insecure. Of course, these children hadn't caused their mother's anger. It was there long before they were born.

If this woman had been my client—and she was not—I would have explained to her that her trauma was not her fault. However, it was her problem. I would have told her it was up to her—like it is up to all of us—not to settle for stuck. It is up to us to find our way to release ourselves from The Model, reconnect with our knowing, retake charge of our lives. No one can do that for us. We must do that for ourselves. Someone had broken this woman somewhere along the way to the point where she could not bring herself to process her trauma and reclaim her life. Naturally, her children took the trauma of a childhood under her rule into their adulthood. However, at least a few of them believed they deserved better and took on the task of freeing themselves from their trauma.

I relate to that. Maybe you do, too. For me, it took wild endurance to move through my life once I could see that the majority of us—including me, at that time—were lying to ourselves. Many of the people I lived among were like that woman, uninterested in going inward and looking at themselves. Once I began to look at myself, however, and find some healing in that process, I found I had to leave many relationships in order to feel safe and to complete my healing. Once I could hear my knowing, I could trust that it knew who to move me away from and who to move me toward.

While getting into the details of my life has caused me pain, it also revealed to me how things work. I don't need to be anything or to achieve anything to be in my knowing. Though I see that everything is possible for me, whatever comes to me in this lifetime is fine. Whatever doesn't is also fine. In knowing, we can release ourselves from "having to have" or yearning for. We move into an approach that says however our life unfolds is okay. And whatever unfolds, we can meet it not with elation or emotion but with a deep knowing that flows naturally from us—relieved of excuses, blame, or fear of rejection. We do so because we recognize it as our life.

Our culture is at the beginning of seeing there is a Model and taking personal action to change it. You and I are setting the tone for how this becomes second nature for us and for others. It is up to us—and every individual on this journey with us—to find where we fit and to reveal the power in who we are. As I have said before, the way I do this will not be the way you do it. All I can be—all this book is meant to be—is a guide rail to help you see The Model so you can find your way free of it. Though this takes a lot, I know you came into the world ready for it. It requires that you keep open to possibility, move into expectancy and responsiveness, break down rules keeping you stuck, and move away from those who cling to these rules. When you make a mistake in this process—and you will—you now know to allow the natural consequence of that action to inspire your thinking.

I don't believe we fully create our life. I believe we are sent to this life knowing the job we have to do, and now is our time to do it. If you've made it to this chapter, you understand that you are the ultimate authority in your life. You understand that all you need to live your life free from fear, doubt, and worry is to step out of The Model, break its tethers and false connection, and open the channels back to yourself. You also realize that when it comes to your knowing, only you can lead the way for you; only you can be your teacher.

YOU AS YOUR TEACHER

Positioning ourselves as the authority in our own lives is something most people rarely take the opportunity to do—preferring The Model's pseudo-certainty and regurgitated facts over natural curiosity and expansive experiential evidence. However, while allowing The Model to fill in the blanks might feel easier and safer in the short run, in the long run—which you are likely experiencing right now—it leaves you feeling uneasy, misunderstood, and yearning.

As your own teacher, the most difficult subject on your syllabus is gaining that self-trust we talked about in Chapter 5. You want trust that is strong enough to empower you to let your curiosity lead and keep you moving forward with what, at times, might seem like a dimly lit lamp. You want a trust in yourself that supports you as you embrace the process of your life and go with your knowing, confident it is taking you where you need to be. If you can teach yourself to trust like that (and it takes effort), the rest comes easily. Life itself will provide the opportunities you need to deepen your relationship with your knowing. As we've discussed, sometimes your knowing will feel irrational, or at the very least, discombobulated. But if you can learn to move through the fear and into the vulnerability and self-expression, you will put yourself on a trajectory to a fulfilled state.

NO RULES

Being our own teacher does not mean we don't listen to others. It means we consistently put the teachings and tools we encounter from outside sources (like this book!) through the filter of our own knowing. And we expand our thinking by challenging new information and waiting to see what arrives to inform us further. We get in trouble when we adopt others' words, ideas, and rules without question instead of integrating only what works for us. There is no one way to live, no one way to reconnect to our knowing. Whatever arrives for you, use your knowing to take what you need from it in that moment and leave the rest.

While we might not require a special practice to be in touch with our knowing, when you have lived deep in The Model for decades and find you are unsure of yourself, activities such as meditation, journaling, or a spiritual practice can help you clarify your thoughts. I have made myself available to many traditions, therapies, and practices that have helped me get closer to myself and my knowing. For me, each is a tool—not a way of life. We are on this earth to live, not to adhere to rituals. I use a practice when I need to work through certain states of being. For example, meditation tends to calm me down and journaling helps to break my resistance and pull the negativity off my thinking. Exercise also calms me down, while verbal processing gives me clarity. However, I only use these tools as needed.

You likely will need some kind of support during this process. So, if you find an activity or practice that works for you, use it. Just don't let it cause drama or pain in your life. You'll know you are posturing in The Model if you need to defend it. There is a fine line between doing something to get the results you seek and pushing through a practice thinking it's "the thing"—and allowing it to replace questioning what you are experiencing and facing head-on what is distressing you internally. As we've discussed, with most things in life, if you ask yourself (your knowing) if the thing you are doing is for you and you don't sense a "yes," then the answer is "no."

We humans spend a lot of time trying "to be good" instead of being ourselves. Give things a chance, but do not get attached. You can let go of a meditation practice and still call on the energy from your best meditation experience. Hanging on to any practice, operating for perfection, or defending your practice can signal fear. Such signals let you know you are in The Model. Be open-eyed about the variety of healing methods available to you and tune in.

When you head in a direction not meant for you, you might feel anxiety or notice vocal fry (which demonstrates trauma toward creating) when you speak about it. You might find yourself questioning things you didn't question before. When that's the case, ask yourself why that's happening. Doing so moves you closer to your knowing over time. Maybe the direction you're heading is bringing up things that need processing (such as traumas), or maybe it simply is not the right direction for you. Sort through it and find your answers.

In the end, there is no one prescribed way to reconnect to your knowing. Whenever we decide that life, our goals, our dreams have rules we must adhere to, we start to control ourselves or others. When it comes to knowing, there are no rules. Only your way for you. And my way for me. The faster we ditch the rules and use pure curiosity and creativity to learn to navigate our lives with our knowing, the more quickly we build our lives on a foundation of truth—opening the way for more trust and connection.

Your journey back to your knowing is about being able to see and accept what is for you alone. It takes making choices and maintaining active attention to how you are living. Does it always feel good? No. Is it an error-free path? Never. But as you see results, experience natural consequences, and begin to feel more comfortable in your life, you build an understanding of how this works for you. Those natural consequences help remind you what to move away from and where to go deeper. They also naturally remove you from trying to put yourself in the hierarchy. Your success will be in not shrinking, not mentally justifying, and not philosophizing the pain. You must allow the emotions to flow to get to the heart of the matter.

What I have seen over the years is most people move out of The Model and into their knowing the way they're built. If you are feisty and fierce, you may move through this like a passionate bucking bronco. If you are by nature easygoing and mild, that may be how you do it. At some point, you will be angry. That anger—simply the breakdown of unexpressed feelings—will drive the change and action leading you to you.

RECOGNIZE YOUR PATTERNS

As I have alluded to throughout this book, our lives unfold in patterns. Our knowing springs from anticipating what is next based on the pulse of a pattern. Patterns color everything. They are the constant our knowing ensures and are sensed more than seen. They can reveal our knowing to us when we allow it. Everybody on earth acts according to patterns, whether they are aware of them or not. When you act out of patterns that are natural to you, you act in ways that serve you best. When you act out of The Model's patterns, you act in ways that disserve you and only serve The Model. As you grow stronger in your knowing, you sense the difference more easily and intensely.

Daniel Kish, for example, did not resist his nature. He followed his natural patterns to be who he was and is—and therefore fulfilled his need. His choices to echolocate, live fully, and start a foundation to help others with impaired vision do the same, illustrate why our natural patterns are both essential and unique to us. They lead us to our full expression of ourselves—not a compromised pattern that can hurt others, create untrue or unhealthy bias (judgment and projection), or destroy our true human ability and rightful desire to connect.

My natural patterns were always there, gnawing at me. They didn't appear to necessarily relate specifically to me but more to how we as humans live against who we are instead of flowing with it. Even when I tried to avert my attention, these patterns were there to direct and teach me. Once I opened myself to them, I found myself expressing a truer and fuller self—unbound by The Model. I see this in my clients as well. Often after our first session, they tell me, "I feel so much better. I've never thought of it this way or had anywhere I could discuss this before." "This" being a deeper philosophical understanding of our world, why things are the way they are now, of their fears that for so long have gone unspoken, and of their knowing. It is amazing how much sense it makes for them once they can see it.

Our natural patterns are our cue that our knowing is always there, offering support beyond our imagination. If we allow it, our natural patterns can provide us with the confidence and certainty to relieve our lives of drama that drags us down and keeps us stuck. They release us from the bonds of hierarchy. They lead us away from judgment. They lead us into an equality with the world and other people. They move us into distributed abundance. When we trust in our natural patterns and the behaviors and knowing that emerge from them, there is a solid shift in how we show up in our lives and where we release control and embody power.

MODEL-DERIVED PATTERNS

While our natural patterns guide us to our knowing and an expression of our true selves, The Model's patterns are trying to coerce us into their conforming behaviors. If we are not alert, our fears and traumas can cause us to suppress our natural patterns (and thus, our knowing and genuine expression of ourselves) to make room for The Model's influence over us, leading to false expression or posturing.

When you are in one of The Model's posturing patterns, you express behaviors to manipulate a situation or another person. For instance, if you notice yourself boasting, proving, telling, or withholding information from someone, you are likely in The Model's authoritarian posture and expressing patterns to directly control another person, as we discussed in Chapter 2.

When you "boast," what you are really saying to someone else is, "I'm better than you"—with the hope of creating a false hierarchy that gives you control. "Telling" means, "I know better than you"—again establishing a false pecking order. "Proving" typically translates into, "My truth is the truth, so no need for you to question it or assert your version of it"—with The Model's hope here being that neither the other person nor yourself will question or go any deeper with it. And when you "withhold or avoid information," what you are really doing is undercutting the other person's ability to accurately know what's going on. All of them are an attempt for control, for the false certainty The Model dangles in front of you.

In the same vein, if you find yourself expressing worry, drama, guilt, or are, again, withholding but in a more subtle way, you are likely taking The Model's less obvious posturing patterns for control—enabling, also discussed in Chapter 2. Though these tactics may elicit more sympathy, they are just as manipulative. "Worry" says, "I don't believe in you." "Guilt" expresses, "Either you or I or both of us will never be good enough." "Drama" espouses, "I take offense to this situation—though I do nothing to correct it." Drama avoids facts in order to build fear. And "withholding" on the enabling side of The Model is an attempt to prevent others from gaining their own clarity on a situation—clarity that might lead them to a conclusion outside The Model. All of these patterns signal false power and rely on placing you as knowing better for someone than they know for themselves. You are disallowing that their choices and consequences are theirs.

Most devastating, however, is all seven of these behavior patterns prevent you and others in your life from finding solutions, making true connections, and being honest with yourself. I have done them all. You may also have done them all. We have seen these behavior patterns in other people. Now that we can recognize them, we can use this knowledge as a flare. When these patterns show up, we can use them to make us aware that it is time to go inward and figure out what we really want and how we get back to being who we truly are outside of The Model.

Expressing on patterns that are not natural to you do nothing for anyone, including yourself. It breaks us down, makes us a shred of who we are, and leaves us feeling stuck. The result is frustration, and in severe cases, feelings of desperation. We see this throughout society today—people behaving in desperate ways and expressing themselves through extreme posturing. No longer able to think for themselves— yet still hungry for expression—they become obsessive. The Model drives them to need to be "right," to prove their place and value in The Model's hierarchy. The Model then affirms and encourages this choice by giving them a false sense of connection to others expressing the same misguided pattern. These people shrink from curiosity and stick to judgment, which turns into grievance. They get caught in a corner of needing to believe in one extreme thing or person and lose themselves.

In contrast, when we step into our knowing, we step into our nature and behave accordingly. Our nature is not to violate others or avoid consequences. Our nature does not need to "prove" or be "right." Our nature is to be curious about this life, to try things out, to make mistakes sometimes, and to learn. So if we find ourselves around people who are in an extreme pattern from The Model and posturing, we need to recognize that and make powerful choices about how this affects us. If we find ourselves reacting to their posturing (outwardly or inwardly), we need to take a break from that relationship. The Model tells us taking a break is not okay. However, if our aim is to be Model-free, it becomes your pathway to freeing yourself. As always, be especially aware not to be burdened by others' anger. We need to let the energy they put into the world return to them so that they can feel the consequences of it. This is the way narcissism collapses.

By bringing our awareness to the patterns we express—especially when we are feeling frustrated—we can identify if they are natural to us or a product of The Model. We can use that knowledge to align with our knowing and ourselves. As always, acting to rid your life of The Model means possibly being out of favor with others. You might even "look bad" to them. However, you know that by exchanging the energy of posturing patterns for patterns that are natural to who you are—and you know you are doing so because you have nothing to defend or sell others—you live a life true to what is and leave behind the stifling world of what isn't.

PATTERN TRACKING AND RECONCILING

You can make yourself more aware of the patterns in your life simply by observing them. For a time, I kept a spreadsheet identifying the work I did with my inner child parts, which hold a key to our patterns. My therapist at the time said, "Well, that is not how we do it." I laughed and said, "That's how I do it." I identified how each inner child pattern made me feel. I noted how I physically and emotionally felt—how my body responded and signaled—in different situations and with different people. The more I brought my patterns into the forefront, the more I recognized the points at which I felt best. I became grateful by nature. Even when I was among those who did not expand me, I saw that knowing who I am allowed me to naturally keep the emotional distance needed to continue to operate fully as myself. With this self-knowledge, I encouraged my learning and growth, moving myself closer to where my power resides. I dealt with things head-on as they arrived. I watched the patterns play out and saw the pulse of how to break free of control. Though at first it unnerved every fiber of my being, I learned to resolve the need to control things that were not mine to control, and instead, follow a more natural arc into my power. Going with my patterns allowed me to flow through situations instead of feeling trapped by them.

Our patterns allow us to reclaim who we are instead of continuing to live a life that is not ours. For instance, while watching a video of myself hanging out with my children in the backyard when they were little, I was horrified at the pattern I saw in the way I interacted with them. I saw for the first time how controlling I was. I was constantly intervening in their play, telling them what to do or not do, replacing their thoughts with mine. I was following a learned parenting technique. I was in The Model.

When I confided in a friend about my behavior toward my children, she immediately justified it. She said I was "just being a protective mom." While I appreciated her trying to make me feel better and, in a way, wanted to agree with her so I could continue in my well-worn, comfortable parenting pattern, I stayed with my knowing. I had to resist letting my friend or The Model tell me that a controlling parent was a "good" or "authoritative" parent (not to be confused with authoritarian). It is not. I knew I was in a pattern that wasn't good for my kids or authentic to who I was or wanted to be for them, and therefore not my natural pattern. I was not sure how to be different. However, I was sure I needed to lead myself to a truer place for me. My awareness of this pattern was the beginning of teaching myself how to leave The Model and to be the parent I knew I wanted to be. As I said, there is no right way to do this or figure this out; there is only your way. Your way is always the most powerful way for you. As you do this, be aware of "well-meaning friends" who are unknowingly steering you back into The Model.

In my life, I use my awareness of The Model's common patterns to change my own behavior. When I see others exhibiting these patterns, I am more aware that perhaps this is someone I might need to move away from in my life. At the very least, I know I need to observe to see if they are a real friend or a relationship worth maintaining. Much as I did after seeing the video of myself interacting with my kids playing in the yard, I need to stay out of the "status quo" way of perceiving relationships and make sure the relationship is true for me—that it is good for me and for the other person as well. Acting on this gives me the opportunity to address emotions, making room for even more clarity. Then on my own, I can revisit what made me feel concerned or uncomfortable about being with this person or people. Taking all of it behind the scenes, I can release resistance and restore myself to who I truly am in my own time, on my own terms. As you do this work, you find yourself attracting people who energize you, who flow better and better with who you truly are.

In general, any pattern you have that has control as its aim is likely a product of The Model trying to control you and keep you stuck in its game. For some, it can look like a need to keep up a life that "looks good"—whether it is good or not. For others, it is being organized to the point no one else can participate in their life. And for too many of us, it is constant anxiety over just about everything. If you don't allow yourself to see The Model's patterns in your life, you can't possibly know the changes you need to make to free yourself from them. There is always an angle being played with somebody in The Model, realized or not.

Inside The Model, insecurity, lack of connection and empathy, and resistance to intimacy cause us to behave in these patterned ways, vying for a sense of control and a better place in The Model's hierarchy. In contrast, our natural patterns, those derived from our knowing, don't make us seek rank or control. When we act on such patterns, our actions are intelligent, considerate, and without judgment. We are free of yearning to be on top, to be regarded outside ourselves as more, to appear different than we are. When we act from a place of knowing, we thrive in a way meant for us.

GETTING CLEAR ON WHAT'S TRUE FOR YOU

If we are to teach ourselves to let go of The Model's patterns in our life, we must listen to ourselves and accept hard truths without judging. We must be willing to stay with our feelings and arrive at our own sense of order. And we must address our inner parts to heal and restore those suppressed expressive parts of our personality we call our shadow. Only we can know our experience.

Acting as my own teacher, I told myself not to react or berate myself for "The Model–type" parenting I saw in that video of my kids and me. At the time, I was aware enough of my knowing to realize I needed to feel the heaviness that resulted from controlling my kids. I needed to allow that discomfort until clarity arrived. And that's what I did. Soon after, two opportunities came my way for me to see my patterns more clearly.

While it was not pleasant, seeing the video and the two opportunities that came my way revealed to me that I was projecting my own hurts and problems on my children—much as my parents had done to me (and probably their parents to them). With that bit of clarity, I could see I had to have the same trust in my children and their knowing that I was working to give myself. If I wanted to nurture emotionally confident, independent children—and I knew I did—my parenting needed to be about guiding them as they made their own choices, not forcing them to adopt what I thought was best. I had to trust their knowing would bring them to consequences that would land them on the right path for them—no matter what it looked like to me in any given moment. I realized parenting was more of an art form than the constant exercise of rules and maintaining order, emotional and otherwise.

For instance, when one of my kids came home from half-day kindergarten and announced, "I'm overwhelmed." My immediate reaction was, "No, you're not. You are five years old. You don't know overwhelmed." But I stopped myself from saying it out loud. I chose to deal with myself later—to get curious about why I felt the need to deny their feelings—behind the scenes. Putting my reaction aside in the moment, I gently asked my child what they could do about it. They responded, "I don't know." It was then my child let go and knew it was safe to feel this way, and I could see the overwhelm on their face and in their eyes. To be the parent I wanted to be, I knew I needed to give my child the opportunity to process. My response—taking them at their word—validated their feelings. They knew I trusted them, helping them to trust themselves. Then, because they expressed that they didn't know what to do with their overwhelm—after all, most five-year-olds don't know what to do with such big feelings—I provided some options, allowing them to make their own choice and retain control over their situation. One option was to read books until they felt ready to join in with the rest of the family. Knowing my child, I knew they would choose reading, and they did. But it would not have mattered which option they chose. Having a choice kept their recovery in their hands and on their terms—which let them know themselves and their needs better. Also, the simple act of offering them a choice told them I trusted in their ability to find their own way through their emotions, which made them trust themselves more at that moment and planted a seed for the future. Within ten minutes, my child was restored and ready to join us. If I had ignored their feelings and let their overwhelm build or never met my child and their autonomy in this way, I'd probably be writing a different book.

The clarity we need is always there within us. We know ourselves even when the distractions and disruptions of modern life obscure our insight or our past haunts us. But we have been conditioned to second-guess. (If you don't believe it, track your patterns to see for yourself if that is something you do.) This conditioning is a stumbling point for most of us. For the clarity we need to reconnect to our knowing fully and to self-govern, we must eliminate second-guessing and the physical and mental activities that distract or stop us from confronting open spaces of emotion and mental activity. Instead, we must put effort toward making the necessary life changes to rid our lives of anything that perpetuates The Model.

Identifying and changing behavior patterns can feel like a repetitive and sometimes annoying process. Again, be patient with yourself and move through it your way. Different things are likely to work at different times to shift the patterns, ultimately moving you into trust and preemptive boundaries with others. Expect it to take time. This process rarely occurs in an instance, with a single new insight or revelation—but it can happen like that. If you sense something is off, something is. Heed it.

It took me years of paying attention to my parenting patterns to break the need to control. Slowly, I became adept at calling myself out for ruminating on the "shoulds" of parenting and returning to what I knew (and wanted) for my relationship with my children. In time, this inside change showed outwardly in my behaviors. People—including my former husband—called me a "magic parent." But it was no magic. It was quietly hard-won trust in myself and them, and it changed everything for all of us.

Give yourself the space you need for clarity. When you can see what is really happening and understand the whys of your patterns, the trust in your knowing comes easier—and that expands your perspective, reveals your potential, and presents you with the opportunity to make your life and relationships exactly as you want them to be. Stay aware that processing emotions can be exhausting and frustrating at times. Don't be afraid to ask for help. If nobody says "yes" to helping you, accept that this is a moment where you can do it on your own, even if it feels hard, even when it feels impossible.

To ensure my clients have ongoing support, I manage an online community. We meet once a month online, talk, and explore where we are with our knowing. (You can learn more about it at www.amyvasterling.com.) Whether or not this is right for you, I encourage you to find and join a supportive group of people who are open to transformation in their own lives and are moving in the same direction you are heading in. Perspective and support are key as you move out of The Model and into your knowing.

CHANGING YOUR PATTERNS CHANGES YOU

Being more and more Model-free in my parenting made me more confident and powerful in all areas of my life. As my parenting patterns changed to favor my knowing and not The Model, my relationship to myself changed. For instance, I felt a nudge to become a public speaker—something I had never considered before, something that terrified me, something I would have talked myself out of when I was out of touch with my knowing. But now, believing in myself, in my knowing, I paid attention to that nudge. I trusted that this was meant to be a next step for me, and I opened myself to accepting whatever came with it or of it.

Interestingly, some opportunities to speak came my way. For one of my earliest speaking engagements, I found myself in front of seventy-five people, which, at the time, was a lot of people. I was nervous. But as I spoke, I could feel the expression of who I truly am coming through. I could feel what I was saying connecting with the audience.

After the talk, lots of people came up to ask questions and express their appreciation. Two women stood out to me. One told me, "I don't know why, but I want to touch you," and then she grabbed my arm. The other lambasted the way I presented myself. At home later, thinking about these two women, it came to me that they summed up my experience exactly. Part of me had felt powerful standing in front of all those people to connect with them on an important message—my message. Part of me felt wobbly, like who was I to expect people to care about what I think (and know)? The toucher was physically expressing that connection to me, what my knowing was leading me toward. It felt like she could sense my potential but not yet articulate it—just like me in that moment. The criticizer was The Model and the shame and disconnection that results from it. I learned that taking an opportunity to connect—even through something as scary as public speaking—was stronger in me than the fear of shame. Stepping out of my old Model pattern, following in my knowing's new patterns, led me to connection with a broader swath of people than I had ever known. I wasn't a perfect speaker. I wasn't unafraid. It was connection that gave me the confidence I needed. Confidence I could now depend on. My knowing was expanding me and what was possible for me, and it felt good.

As my own teacher, I built on this experience. I used it to strengthen my trust in my personal knowing. I clung to it whenever uncertainty tried to drive fear into me. I leaned into it to allow myself to be vulnerable, act as I was meant to, and finally, let go of the fear and The Model. When I identified something that felt broken inside me, I used it to figure out where I might need healing. When I felt myself in a neutral response, I knew I was on the right path for me.

Today, I regard any feeling of worry, fear, or shame as signs The Model is trying to creep back into my life and coax me into straying from what I know. When I find myself back in patterns that demonstrate my disconnection from my knowing (like I get preachy or overly quiet or suddenly feel anxious), I immediately recognize them. I no longer see my discomfort as a problem; I see it as a signal alerting me that something is off—such as I'm interacting with someone who is not healthy for me or doesn't see me as who I am. By recognizing what is not working and trusting the power to know for myself, trauma is naturally dispelled. My knowing knows who is for me and who is not.

My life as I write this book is uncertain, yet it makes me happy. My life is in a period of big unknowns. I'm newly divorced. My children are grown with their own lives—a huge change for any parent. As a constant traveler, I'm not sure where in the world (literally) or when I'll have a home base again. It is not a life I had the skill to live in my twenties. It is only made possible by becoming the authority of my own life, looking out for behavior patterns that do not serve me, and then using my personal knowing to align my behaviors with who I am and what I want. I challenge you right here and now to commit to being your own teacher, to seeing your true reactions based on how others treat you, to figuring out what you will defend and why. The next time you feel something is off, I challenge you to feel no need to act in the moment, to put it aside until you can take your emotions and resistance behind the scenes and resolve the pattern yourself. Needless to say, these things take practice.

Once you feel it resolve within, you'll know you've mastered the pattern. Sometimes other people in our lives shift with us, and sometimes they don't. Let go! Wanting them to shift with you is The Model's definition of love. Real love is letting everyone find their way and go their way.

At points in this process, you might find a pattern that keeps coming around again and again, feels like it keeps you stuck, and is particularly challenging to change. Those times call you to have the most trust in yourself. But whatever happens, be assured that knowing is a fluid experience. If you don't catch or can't change something the first or millionth time, there will be plenty more chances. Natural consequences will arrive. Model-laden people will amplify their intensity, or new people will enter your life. All of this provides you with opportunities to overcome obstacles and reevaluate the patterns you keep inside and act on outwardly. Also, knowing is nonlinear, non–time-bound. Expand with it. Go with it. Keep with it, and your power and wisdom will shine for you in ways you never imagined.

As you move away from The Model and toward proficiency with your knowing, you change the forces that have pushed and pulled you through life so far. Thus, by nature, you move into a new way of being—your way of being. While this process can be trying, in the end you'll see—and trust even more in—how it drives clarity and choices for you to be you if you follow it.

NEVER STOP LEARNING

By avoiding trends and teaching yourself, you mitigate outside voices that might get you to second-guess yourself. You recognize the patterns that do and do not work for you more confidently and readily and connect them to your emotions. As I've said, inner child work is the core of recognizing these inside patterns that influence our outward behaviors—particularly our fearful ones. Understanding and reclaiming these inner parts as part of your personality allows for your full expression. When you take time to process them, you—like all the best educators—transform your student (you) from being what you are told to be to becoming who you are. As you take charge of yourself and the old patterns fall away, your knowing gets louder and stronger. When it does get quiet at points, you can remain secure enough in your knowing to wait for it to come to you again. Remember that you are a front-runner in this process. In time, I believe all human beings will restore operating this way, but for now, you are out in front of most people, forging the way forward.

Your journey to reclaim your knowing may not be easy, but it is well worth it. Problems that once overwhelmed you become easy to solve. The more you restore your knowing, the more every aspect of your life aligns with who you innately are and are meant to be. Your true value system is revealed. Integrity guides you. Drama subsides. Emotionally, your life is no longer a series of ups and downs. Thus, you have room and energy to find your creativity, fearlessness, and your own wild edge that separates you from the pack. With confidence, you navigate your life, knowing and easily accepting things will work out as they are intended—even big things like a loved one's passing. In time, your ego (a negative by-product of The Model) recedes. And with nothing to prove, your wisdom kicks in full throttle. During the process, this may feel like a bumpy road. Hang in there. Acknowledge your emotions, feel them, learn from them, and then let them go.

Teaching yourself to identify and change lifelong patterns, release control, and heal from the inside out is going to be challenging. But if we rerun The Model's patterns for our life, we stay stuck and nothing changes. Every lesson you teach yourself prepares you for the next. Every cycle of growth leads to a deeper wisdom—with fewer negative consequences and more opportunities to experience who you truly are.

Chapter Eight

RELATIONSHIP EVOLUTION

Throughout our lives, our relationships help us define how we see ourselves and the world we live in. They shape us, our decisions, and our behavior. When we are very young, our relationships consist mostly of family members, the most impactful usually being our relationship with our parents. As we grow, we choose our friends. Thus, our relationships reflect the values and priorities we have established. If we've spent the majority of our lives stuck in The Model, our relationships will reflect that—making them less likely to be as supportive as we try to free ourselves and return to our knowing.

Redefining and sometimes culling existing relationships is one of the most difficult tasks for my clients as they reconnect to their knowing. Throughout this book, we've discussed how living in our knowing returns us to our expression at the core of who we are and ultimately frees us from judging and being judged. This return requires making decisive changes in ourselves and how we engage with our world. Relationships with people who insist on our adhering to The Model often grow distant or fall away. The relationships that stay are those that evolve with our knowing. We also find new relationships that support our knowing. Some of this happens naturally. Some painfully. All of it with heightened awareness on our part and a deepening of our relationship with ourselves.

Fully living in our knowing sometimes means eliminating, or with open eyes, managing, relationships in our lives that want us to remain in The Model and try to keep us from being who we are—either causing us to behave poorly or, likely, go with unmet emotional and other needs. Only you can see your relationships for what they are to you. Only you can know which to keep and which to let go. Just make sure you aren't hanging on to them because of fear.

THE RELATIONSHIPS WE LEAVE

When I started talking about my move to Europe, many people told me they would visit once I got settled. Most, of course, were just making polite conversation and had no intention of following through. But hearing this over and over again got me thinking about who I'd be glad to see at my door and who I'd be glad remained an ocean away. In other words, which relationships would encourage my knowing and which would unknowingly hold me back from who I was becoming—me.

The people I didn't want making that trip all had one thing in common: They were judgmental of my choice to go in the first place. Though most said nothing to me directly, all let me know in one way or another that they did not approve of my decision. Some shared they were "concerned" about me making such a dramatic change so soon after leaving my marriage. Others suggested my being alone in a foreign country was "inviting danger." And many took passive-aggressive aim at what they thought would be my biggest area of vulnerability—being far away from my children, which they expressed as "leaving my children." Of course, they all knew my children were adults who had already left my home, had their own lives in college and beyond, and were fully capable of getting hold of me whether I was in Minnesota or Madrid. They may have been saying things like, "You're so brave. I could never leave my children," but I could feel what they really meant was, "How dare you go outside The Model and the code of motherhood." They were trying to pull me back into The Model, trying to coerce me into what they considered more "normal" or "mainstream" behavior. For them, everything would have been a lot more comfortable if I had simply lived up to The Model's expectations for me and not chosen to live by the nature of who I knew myself to be. However, I don't think I would have survived much longer not being me.

Be prepared: You may find yourself ending, or putting strict boundaries around, a lot of relationships. If you've spent a lifetime feeling "different" than others, you are likely a leader in this movement and just as likely will find yourself reevaluating more of your relationships than those who do not feel "different." You may find that many of the people in your life won't like you reconnecting with your knowing because it challenges their thinking (their perceived comfort in The Model) and what to expect from you, making them fearful. Some of these people will leave you. Some—as my own experience showed—will work to entice you back into The Model by judging your actions and planting doubt, notably doing the same things that put you into The Model in the first place. For instance, if you tell them you had a rare opportunity of a last-minute ticket to an event that was hard to get a ticket to and went, instead of saying, "How exciting! Tell me all about it," they might comment, "Well, it must be nice." If you tell them you've decided to quit your job and start your own business, they will give you a million reasons why it is imprudent and won't work—"You'll lose your house," "You are about to put children through college," "Who would pay for your services?"—or whatever roadblock to your clarity they can find.

Make no mistake, statements such as, "I know you better than you know yourself," or "I know better for you than you know for your-self"—implied or directly said—are only about control. Rarely does anyone say these things to encourage you to be you and to go ahead and act on your knowing. Almost always, these nonsensical statements are followed by advice to do what is conventional, to meet The Model's expectation, because they believe The Model to be the least risky, most secure way to a happy life. Just to be clear: It is not.

When I examined those who landed in the category of people I did not want a visit from, I saw my relationship with them had become more of a crutch than an inspiring connection in which I could find encouragement to grow and evolve as a human being. With some, I shared a history and not much more. These people needed me to meet their expectations more than they wanted me to be me, which went both ways. I wanted them to meet my expectations, causing us both to posture in The Model more than share true connection. It was a match for no one, and, in time, only harmed us both. The truth here for me is they needed me to be less than I am—which led me to see I did not need them.

You probably already notice that the more you act from your know-ing, the more tense your relationships with "Model people" become. You find yourself being scolded or having to hold your tongue in their presence. The more entrenched they are in The Model, the more likely they are to be agitated by your acting in alignment with your knowing. Triggered by what they regard as your nonsensical and even rebellious choices, they lash out in hopes of getting you to realize your error. Some may use passive-aggressive words and actions to get you back into The

Model. Some are directly hostile. Though you might feel insulted or hurt, they likely don't regard what they are doing as malicious or undermining. If asked, they would explain their behavior as simply "telling you like it is," "saving you from yourself," or "being real." To them, it's "helping," but you know it is only saying, "Get back in The Model."

What is real is that their attacks and negativity, subtle or overt, are motivated by their own fear. Your independence and willingness to follow your knowing wherever it takes you threaten them because it forces them to question their own life choices. Your choosing to confidently believe in what you know challenges everything they think they know—The Model. If they accept you and your knowing, they must lose their belief in The Model's certainty, and thus, its false sense of security. That is scary. So instead of trusting that you know for yourself and learning by your example, maybe realizing that they can trust in themselves, they lash out or scold (to the degree it creates discomfort) because they need to feel certain again. They think that can only be achieved through The Model's control of themselves and everyone else. They don't believe it can come through honesty, and they have no self-awareness to see themselves in this lie.

But your knowing is not about them (which they also find threatening). The mere act of operating from your knowing removes your dependence on them and The Model. In this way, you break the cycle. If the majority of our species moves in this direction, narcissism will cease altogether, and the freedom that knowing brings will be observed and lived by each of us.

CATHEXIS VS. ETERNAL LOVE

Here's a hard truth: Having a healthy, mutually respectful relationship with someone stuck in The Model is not possible. Whether a parent, sibling, romantic partner, or friend, people who heed or trust in The Model regarding your relationship to them do not have the capacity to care without condition. This is because of the unseen hierarchy. What The Model demands always comes before what the other person in the relationship wants or needs for themselves. Often it is challenging to see this is happening, which supports The Model rejecting the opportunity for growth. Even when both parties are in The Model, a power differential remains—and the advantage always goes to The Model.

In his 1978 bestseller, *The Road Less Traveled*, psychiatrist M. Scott Peck compares the concept of "cathexis" to "love." He defines cathexis as being invested in or obsessed with an object or person. He explains that such a relationship is "only satisfactory as long as their will coincides with ours." Thus, it is a relationship that fosters dependency. In contrast, he defines love (imperfectly, he admits) as "the will to extend one's self for the purpose of nurturing one's own or another's spiritual growth." He includes "self-love" within that definition.[9] I'll add that connection to our knowing leads us to self-love. Understanding ourselves and our purpose free of fear moves us into self-expression. The ultimate gain is we move out of the "spiritual" and into a new perception about ourselves as the creator.

When we are in The Model, many of us confuse cathecting with loving—especially when we are young and dependent on adults for our survival. We might say our parents "loved" us because they took good care of us, hugged us, and told us they "loved" us. But if their approval and affection for us were dependent on our meeting their (The Model's) expectations for us—and not on our becoming the full expression of ourselves—their feelings for us were conditional, were used to control us (and maybe still do), and so leaned more toward cathexis than

9   M. Scott Peck, *The Road Less Traveled: A New Psychology of Love, Traditional Values, and Spiritual Growth*, 25th Anniversary ed. (Simon & Schuster, 2002), 81-82, 94, 108.

love. The same goes for our spouses, our friends, and anyone in our lives who threaten to withhold themselves from us if our needs, choices, and actions don't meet with their approval. Such relationships keep us scared and playing small in our lives. They keep us from realizing our true potential and feeling stuck as we operate on a cycle of behaviors we have learned instead of acting on who we are.

Consequently, people living by The Model can cathect you but cannot love you. Their objective is control. They might say, "I love you." They might even think they do. But if they were able to dig a little deeper (and they are not), they would see their relationship with you is all about meeting their needs; yours are not considered. They are interested in you being who they need you to be, not in your growth or expansion—spiritual or otherwise.

Love, or what I like to call "eternal love," encourages and welcomes uninhibited, unattached, free expression, and expansion for everyone. Eternal love has no beginning, no end, and no demands placed on it. It frees us from obsession because there is no possession involved. Eternal love stems from the same place within us from which knowing comes. Thus, it is not charged. But like our knowing, it is neutral—free of ego and shadow.

For most of your life, you got the message not to be yourself—to follow The Model instead. You likely had to heed this message to keep the peace in your household and survive. Perhaps those you were dependent on upped the ante by using physical, psychological, or emotional abuse to keep you in line. Now, with the clarity of your knowing, you are moving beyond that—beyond cathexis—and into eternal love as you choose who you allow in your life. Also important to note is that letting go of relationships can be an act of real love. In this space, you can be as you were meant to be. And those you are in relationship with can be who they are, too. With this comes massive freedom.

Simply put, there is no yearning for eternal love because we understand intuitively that it already exists without need of evidence. When we fully embody this, we don't obsess or look for love because that only signals we are in The Model. We either currently know eternal love within or fully trust that we'll come to understand and embody eternal love as we move more into our personal knowing and our power. From my observation, only a very small percentage of people understand eternal love. The Model and unacknowledged hierarchy give no example of it because eternal love creates a balance of power in place of inequality. This inequality causes us to fight, judge, control. Eternal love, on the other hand, causes us to understand each other. There are few—possibly no—examples of what eternal love is because it evades drama. Hollywood's romantic films all depict The Model's version of love. Because of the intensity of our exposure to The Model's version of love in the media and in most of the relationships we see around us, it is challenging to know how to love differently.

CATHEXIS AND CARE

Cathexis is held up or justified by care. Care as an outgrowth of eternal love can be a supportive kindness that helps another and shows them they are seen and loved. Care that is an outgrowth of The Model (which is more often the case) assumes "doing things others will like." In other words, the person providing the care is not asking the other person what they need or want. They are giving what they like, what they prefer, or what they assume the other person should have—overriding the other's needs and who they actually are. It is authoritarian or enabling behavior. The enabler tries hard to anticipate another's need with the goal of not only being seen as "good" but also through that "goodness" controlling the receiver with their kindness. The authoritarian aims for outright control, which can quickly turn into gaslighting or conflict that usually ends up repressed by the recipient to "keep the peace" or "not appear ungrateful." Not only is no one aware of themselves in these situations, but no real care is given or received.

I once watched a woman accept a gift from her partner. As she opened it, I could see by her expression that the gift didn't speak to any aspect of her. Not who she was. Not what she liked. Not what she needed. Instead of setting her partner straight, she graciously thanked them for the gift—as The Model teaches all of us to do. She set the gift down on a side table by the couch, and there it sat until it found its way deep into a corner of the closet for years, idle and unseen—just like her.

When our "care" seems unwanted, we can feel threatened and misunderstood. However, before we assume that what we are doing is "care," we need to ask the person we want to care for what it is they want, what would be helpful to them. In a cathexis relationship, each partner wonders if anything they do will ever be enough. Will they ever meet their partner's needs? The answer is to remove The Model. If both are willing to remove The Model from the mix, they can see what is true in the relationship because their traumas and shadows will also be revealed and therefore can be healed.

Real care comes from mutual respect and communication. It helps us receive what works for us. The idea that we sacrifice ourselves for another is not real. In my case—and maybe yours—I sacrificed many years of my life being put in situations that were contrary to who I am to benefit another. I allowed myself to be plunked into something that did not fit who I was—jobs that didn't use my talents, social obligations that truly were obligations, and a marriage that proved stifling for both of us. Over the years, I could feel the intensity grow until I could not hold onto this life that was not mine any longer. I used to say to my then husband that what we were living was not "my life." It took leaving to see why. There is not a chance he would have been happy living what is now my life, nor I what is now his life.

So, when cathexis is at play (which it is more often than not) and our partner, friend, or family member cares for us, they might believe they are caring for us out of love. However, when their care is what they choose to do—and they do not consider or listen to our real needs—it is not love. It is self-validation. It is a way to pretend the relationship is "good" and connection has been made without having to open themselves up to the vulnerability of true connection, of actually knowing another human being and being known yourself. It is a desire to keep the peace by hiding the lie rather than to get to the truth. When we stop believing the perceived power of enabling and stop feeding the authoritarian inside us, we can heal ourselves and find true connection.

THE RELATIONSHIPS WE KEEP

Of course, I did not get rid of all the relationships in my life when I left for Europe. Those friends I truly hoped would visit shared certain traits in common with me: a mutual respect with no judgment or thought of or need to put our expectations on one another. Not coincidentally, the more I connected to my knowing, the more these friendships strengthened and deepened. Whether I had been in them for a long time or had once regarded them as fringe, each took on greater importance to me. So I found they easily ebbed and flowed with my life and mine with theirs. Also, once I started traveling, I seemed to attract people I could connect to almost immediately. Honestly, it makes sense. Showing up in the world as the unique expression of yourself makes it a lot more likely that you will attract people who appreciate you as you are and vice versa.

The relationships we keep are the ones that move us forward and encourage us to expand. They do the same for the other person, too. These relationships are easy because there is no attachment to control or expectations (causing anxiety), holding back one's own trauma (causing depression), clinging to certainty, or otherwise. As I found with my children, my belief in them is no longer conscious it simply is. My belief in them is in a place where it never begins and never ends. It is eternal. As we move into this experience, our relationships become easy because they are built on what we know about ourselves and what we accept is honestly true about others—sometimes for better or worse. We act on who we truly are and stop trying to be somebody we are not.

As you become more trusting in your knowing, the relationships you choose to keep will be selected more by sense than consciously weighing pros and cons. As human beings, we are moving to a place where there will be no hard feelings when it comes to the relationships we accept and those we don't because we will all sense more than we think or feel. Relying on sense changes everything. Nothing is more comforting than being yourself with others—the sense of belonging that creates is undeniable. The sad truth is most of us have had little experience with expressing ourselves fully. However, the potential of being seen as who we truly are reveals itself in people you don't know walking up to you on the street and sharing powerful information you need without selling you a story or a religion.

I know what that's like because it's happened to me. I was attending an online event with five hundred other people. Over several days, I got to know many other attendees while working in various breakout sessions. I sensed a connection to two of those people, and we shared our contact information. Both were receptive when I followed up; however, I knew from those initial interactions that one would fade out of my life right away and one would stay longer and become a friend for a time. And that's what happened. The ability to sense which relationships are "for us" brings us into a natural equality with others—evading the need for judgment, questioning, and second-guessing. You either know that it is or is not for you.

THE POWER OF BELIEVING IN OTHERS

When we truly and freely believe in others, we empower their choice for a life outside The Model. Uninhibited by judgment (positive or negative) and with no fear of impacting the relationship, they feel free to go with what they know and to deal with the natural consequences that may come. As we've discussed, those consequences are necessary. They teach and allow us to live with a greater honesty about who we are. The security of a relationship that allows judgment-free actions and natural consequences lets us feel understood and sure in ourselves and our decisions. It achieves a true place for us to belong uniquely.

People whose choices are persistently questioned by those they are in a relationship with become nervous about making "the wrong" decision, the "disappointing" decision—so they second-guess instead of connecting to what they know. This erring on the side of caution prevents them from accessing their knowing and becoming who they are meant to be. Conversely, when, without thought, we believe in the people in our lives, they grow stronger in trusting themselves. And we grow stronger too—making a better world for everyone. At the same time The Model defines you as weak if you can't believe in yourself, it promotes a kind of self-belief that is more akin to arrogance and is easily recognized as posturing.

Even though we have reconnected with our knowing, we need to understand that we continue to be a work in progress. Reconnecting with our knowing does not mean the ability to hold our tongues and not judge others happens automatically. What does happen is we understand through our sense who expands us and who does not. Therefore, when we are honest about who expands us and move toward them gently, it's obvious and natural who we leave behind or where to place clear boundaries with those who prefer to keep us in The Model. By this action we evade judgment and experience natural equality. When we recognize something irritates us in another, and yet our knowing is clear that we need to be with them, we understand we or they are working their way out of The Model. We also understand it is going to be uncomfortable to witness. And yet, if we live outside The Model, we can trust in our knowing to give us the ability to watch quietly and give their process room to unfold. Observers still working to free themselves from The Model are more likely to judge others who are not as far in the process.

Whatever we think (our mind) or feel (our emotions), we must deal with it behind the scenes. Phrases like "that might not work" or "that sounds risky" only serve to keep us and the other person in The Model. We can go ahead and acknowledge to ourselves that we sense something is off. The next step is for us to get curious in private about our doubts, to ask ourselves what they might be saying to us. Our misgivings are a call for us to listen to (and see) ourselves and get clear with one's self first. We can ask ourselves why what someone said charges us up and reconcile with ourselves if we feel the need to judge them. Once we come to terms with having no attachment to what they do and have only understanding for their pure potential, we can show up for the other person in our full power—free of our own resistance and ready to believe in them and support them as we are able so they can act on what they know is true for them.

For instance, let's say you have a friend who has good ideas but is a bit wild. Some of their ideas have paid off. Some have bombed. When your friend asks you to invest in their latest project, you know it would be too risky for you, so you say no. You do not state any judgment of them, their choices, or their project, knowing that judgment comes from The Model. Instead, you examine your feelings behind the scenes, come to terms with why you feel the way you do, why you think it would be too risky for you, and keep your insights to yourself. You do not give some long, preachy speech about your friend's idea or silently hold judgment against your friend. You accept what they know for themselves. At the same time, you choose not to invest in their project. You believe in them—and you believe in you, too. That's it: no pleasing, no explaining, no judging, no drama. Just a relationship based on respect and support. When we believe in another without condition, we support their expansion. We know natural consequence can step in if they misstep and realign their way forward. And of course we know their life is to be lived and expressed their way. This understanding gives us a great sense of freedom.

To really step away from The Model and nurture relationships that expand with our knowing means continually looking at ourselves behind the scenes whenever we feel triggered. We are not responsible for others' choices and are not here to be told how to live. We can only monitor how we feel about others to get clear on who we can and cannot be for them. Looking within in no way is about regulating yourself. It is about being introspective—to know what parts of The Model may still be triggering you and causing you to want to control instead of having trust in another or letting them go. It also means we listen to others but decide for ourselves and our own life.

Healthy relationships make way for vulnerability to become second nature to us. As you begin to examine the relationships in your life, it may feel like a bit of a revolving door with people coming in and going out. You are simply working through the natural consequences you avoided while in The Model. In time, the only people making it through your door are people who revel in your self-expression, don't regard you as too much, see you as exactly who they have been looking for—and who you feel the same about.

BREAKING FREE

When I was young, I ached so badly to feel love and be among people I understood. Living in The Model as I did, I was dependent on using judgment, not my knowing, to choose relationships. It is all I had seen others in my life do—and I followed in their pattern. So, it is no wonder I struggled to find what I needed from the people around me. Looking back, there were many red flags that I was not with people who were open to letting me be me—my consistent self-questioning and loneliness being some of them. I believe it's time, and the energy is on our side, to speak up and get results. To leave relationships if that is needed to heal and create new relationships that expand us in ways we could not have imagined. As a result, I don't berate myself for not finding more supportive relationships sooner than I did. I don't think that was even possible. I needed what I was dealt to see the underpinnings of the problem, The Model.

Our lives happen in their time. Part of accepting our knowing is accepting that truth. In time, I made changes—small ones, at first—to who I let into my life. What I have learned is when it is time, action, even small action, can move us to healing, to greater self-expression, and ultimately, to fulfillment.

All of us yearn for what we know is true about us to be set into motion. But it is up to us to make it happen, to release our true selves. Only we can choose for ourselves to no longer hide behind The Model's boasting, worrying, withholding, and other postures when in relationships. Only we can let go of, place boundaries around, or take breaks from relationships that don't support our expansion. As you begin this evolution in your own relationships, be prepared for occasional discomfort. Along the way, you may see your clear mind become confused and grotesquely underserve you. You may feel like everything is a bit much. You may discover those you thought brought you joy and comfort do not. But as your internal yearning for your knowing gets louder, you will move to heal what needs healing and find deeper connections in ways you cannot yet understand.

Each of us knows when we cannot continue in a relationship—when the choice becomes continuing to bend to others' expectations for us or honoring what we know. Overthinking our interactions, feeling mental exhaustion, depression (turning against oneself), or experiencing anxiety (attaching to an outcome) after being with someone are signals that a relationship might be more about cathexis than what is eternal. It is up to us to pay attention to these dynamics, to be honest with ourselves, and not to let others keep us in The Model. When you operate from your knowing and understand eternal love for yourself, you can stop looking for relationships. You can trust that those you need will come to you, and in time, they truly do.

Leaving any relationship, or even putting strict boundaries around it—especially with family or longtime friends—takes effort and can hurt. As we have discussed, I knew I needed to release myself from many of the people and places I'd grown up with in order to reconnect with myself. It wasn't easy. Change is generally accompanied by fear. However, we can trust the clarity we gain from our knowing to cut through The Model's drama, address our inner child's fears to heal the shadow, and thereby reclaim ourselves.

I took baby steps with the relationships I found the most challenging to end. Instead of an immediate severing, in some cases, I framed parting ways as "taking a break." Some people were angry with me;

some were agitated—both great signs that the person I was "taking a break" from wanted to control me more than be in true relationship with me. Their responses made it easier to decide which of these challenging relationships I needed to end completely and which I might keep but with better boundaries. Yet it also became apparent to release anybody who didn't fully expand me and I knew who by how safe I felt with them.

Be prepared that you may enter a period where you don't feel connected particularly to anyone or anything. This disconnection is often a sign you are breaking through the status quo and The Model. You are on your way to being yourself and being in harmony with other humans and the world around you. It is a time to make the tough choices. This period is when those clinging to The Model may challenge you or pull away. But the people in your life who are at peace with themselves regarding relating to you will support you. However those around you act, remember that connection is innate, and the closer you move to being you—free of The Model—and the more you feel safe to be vulnerable, the deeper and truer your connections to other people will be.

One good thing about relationships is that the universe won't let you make a bad decision—at least, not for long. If you decide not to terminate a "Model relationship," you can be sure that whatever made you consider getting out of it in the first place won't stop happening. It will come around again and again, escalating each time, until it becomes impossible for you not to choose you.

By letting go of people in your life who are stuck in The Model, you make way for the greatest expression and expansion of your ideas, desires, and who you are, free of control. You also make room for those you let go to do the same. There is no easier or more abundant way to be in the world and no more satisfying way to live than operating from who you truly are with people who know you know best for yourself and love you as you are. We also can appreciate people who know we are "not for them" or who we know are "not for us." With no hard feelings, we can let go. That's eternal love.

YOUR RELATIONSHIP WITH YOU

The most important relationship in your life—the one that defines the quality of all the others—is, of course, the one you have with yourself. As you move further from The Model and closer to who you truly are, that relationship not only intensifies but also becomes more honest. You see yourself for who you are. As your trust in your knowing it continues to grow, you are able to give yourself the same generosity of thought and depth of belief you give to others in your life. The self-sabotage and disparaging voice dissipate.

You also remember each time you struggle to come back to yourself, back within, and take a look at the distance between what you feel now and what it is to be in your power with yourself, or the issue at hand. This introspection helps the pattern shore the gap. Being aware of the feelings and expressing them to yourself lets you release them. Continue the cycle of coming back to you again and again until you clinch acting posture-free and being the true you.

Chapter Nine

KEEPING THE KNOWING FLOWING

n her book *Extraordinary Knowing: Science, Skepticism, and the Inexplicable Powers of the Human Mind,* author and research psychologist Elizabeth Lloyd Mayer writes of events that seem impossible yet have happened on a regular basis in our world. She relates a story about a neurosurgeon with a 100 percent patient recovery rate— almost unheard of in neurosurgery.[10] Unsurprisingly, he is often asked to teach but declines because he "doesn't believe he can teach what he's really doing." What he's doing is sitting with each patient before surgery until "a white light" appears "around his patient's head," signaling to him that it's safe to operate. I'd argue that is his knowing.

Throughout her book, Mayer contends that the neurosurgeon's "white light" experience and other similar phenomena are made

---

10 Elizabeth Lloyd Mayer, *Extraordinary Knowing: Science, Skepticism, and the Inexplicable Powers of the Human Mind* (Bantam, 2007), 11–12.

possible by "unseen powers of the mind." She explains that when she began her study, the concept of "unseen powers of the mind" was foreign to her. However, as she conducted research and gathered data, she found many allies in other scientists and psychologists who had come across this ability in their own research, and, frankly, had seen it in their own lives, and were also hungry to understand it.

What I take from the neurosurgeon's story and the other amazing accounts in Mayer's book is our knowing isn't some mystical, bizarre power. It simply is. My guess is that at first, even that neurosurgeon felt strange sitting with patients (what modern doctor does that?), waiting for his knowing to guide him. But after a few successful surgeries, the pattern was so clear to him that he trusted in his knowing without effort. He didn't need to prove it to anyone. He didn't need to talk about it. The results spoke to him and for him.

That has been my experience with my personal knowing. Those of us who come to trust in our knowing do so because we find it works. As you have read throughout this book, when we permit our knowing to lead us, we experience a pattern of consistent results. Through those experiences, we learn to trust in the pattern itself, no longer needing to know outcomes first. In time, we recognize the positive results our knowing brings to us and its altruistic nature, all without extraordinary effort. We come to experience that trusting in our knowing is more powerful than proving something or making something happen. It's true that maintaining trust can be an ongoing struggle in a culture so tied to The Model, but it is also true that when we allow our knowing to guide us, we live a life with no limits.

Before I fully understood personal knowing, there were times in my life I was calm by nature and naturally following my knowing. But the majority of my adult life I was consciously not following it. Yet, I could still advance in my intuition and use it right out of the box without any tricks. My wisdom still seamlessly shined at times. I am sure you have experienced this, too. Times when you were sure. Times when you felt in the flow with life.

My hope is that you now see that it is possible to live every moment of every day free of the resistance The Model imposes and instead with confidence, with a natural and effortless sense of self and calm that is your true nature. You now realize your knowing is who you are. It is always there for you—more powerful than any anxiety or depression. But it is up to you to live in the steadiness of your knowing, in a state that allows its full expression—and so your full expression.

You are on the brink of creating that life for yourself right now—on your way back to your knowing. You have already begun to turn down the noise of The Model, of gurus, of others telling you how to live. You have started listening to yourself for yourself and for your knowing to guide you once again—because, let's face it, doing so is natural to us.

STAYING IN THE KNOW

Living in your knowing without fear and resistance changes things. It will change you. Be prepared for that. On a personal level, everyday living becomes so much easier without The Model hovering in your mind over every decision you make. On a societal and even global level, as more of us set our Model-free code for navigating life, society as a whole becomes less stressed because there is less stress. As more of us stop participating in The Model's dramas, the world has less drama in it. As our judgment of others diminishes, societal oppression and aggression subside.

But getting there is a journey. Even when you feel the rightness of your knowing at your core, if you are out of the habit of heeding it, you have to put in an effort to not dismiss it when it shows up and not override the potential it offers. At least at first, you need to be deliberate about knowing's simple starting place—about knowing your small preferences and moving onto bigger things. Acting from awareness encourages your knowing because it signals you are remembering to see who you are, rather than denying yourself, as The Model demands.

As you now know, my journey back to my knowing was steep and full of curves. Yours may be, as well. Sometimes I would panic at the deep processing needed to move me free of the past, my shadow, and control. In those times, I needed to remind myself to stay with what I knew—free of any posturing or aim for control. I needed to tell myself that the more I acted on who I am, how I am, and what I know, the more I could let go. Eventually, I more easily exchanged people and places that held me in The Model for things that were true for me and people who supported me. Getting to that place wasn't always easily achieved. I had to let go of The Model's expectations, judgments, and demands on how I live, act, and express myself. But the more I let go, the more my life worked for me and the more you let go yours will work for you too. When I let my knowing guide me, I had more energy, and my fear was replaced by trust.

You, too, will notice that as you allow your knowing to become louder and louder in your life, the chaos will cease. No longer will you have the need to question over and over again what the best choice is for you, what the right choice is. The distress will end and be replaced by a clear trust that allows you to advance, even without all the facts. It is a much easier way to live—maybe even the easiest way to live because it is your way that highlights who you are and, more importantly, what you came to this world to express.

While we may not be able to teach "knowing"—putting rote rules and linear processes on it would be Model-like—we can listen to our own knowing, trust in it, and follow it when making decisions—even if sometimes it doesn't seem to make sense at first, it will in the end. Moving into your knowing is simply attending to the distance between where you are now—what troubles you—and feeling your inherent power to use that troubled feeling to move you toward furthering your growth and the true expression of you. As I have tried to stress, how you do this will be unique to you. But once you feel it, you can let the breakdown begin. You can ease into it, guided by your knowing, letting it show you the way to your power.

Fighting yourself (your knowing) only keeps you in a loop of pain. When you can let go and instead challenge what is holding you stuck, you find release and peace. This is not to say you should trick yourself into positivity and behaving in a way that overrides the depth necessary to explore your strife for what it has to tell you. You must move toward what troubles you so you can move out of it and into your power, trusting that by following your knowing, things will eventually shift your way.

When, for example, you are feeling out of sorts or uncertain, and you find yourself wanting to retreat into the false certainty of The Model, take it as a sign to go deeper inside yourself (deal with yourself behind the scenes) and trust in your knowing. When I experience self-doubt, I challenge myself to let go and trust I'll know what I need as I need it, and I will move through the uncertainty and back to my power. When I find myself forcing a false smile of appreciation, I take it as an opportunity to ask myself where I might be trying to "keep the peace" or what I'm resisting in my current circumstance and why. Whenever our power is restored, we experience freedom and peace, and then a connection opens the way for us to be naturally grateful.

When all goes well—and the more you allow yourself to ditch the fear and face the vulnerability to come back to you—you live a life beyond what you could create in your mind. You live in a world that touches the physical, mental, emotional, and eternal. You experience a life well-lived, expressed, and well-expanded, allowing your uniqueness (something others need) to shine. Acting on our own innate, unique intelligence puts our energy and belief in line and things in our life start to click. We feel flexible where we were not; we flow through change because we accept and feel its purpose even though sometimes we can't put words to what that purpose is until the logic later follows.

MAKE ROOM FOR YOUR LIFE

Once you have solid trust in your knowing, you make choices without the need of a life strategy—which is highly freeing. Now is an unapologetic moment when you get to release what has not worked in your life and make room for what does. Experientially, particularly mentally and emotionally, this can be like walking a tight rope, though. You may have a net below, but you are navigating alone in a powerful way—trusting that you know, believing in yourself, dealing with any wavering as it comes. You might need to grieve some of what you let go of, but you can do so confidently, understanding that in time your life will feel like it is yours and it will operate as such. When that understanding is realized, curiosity naturally usurps judgment—a much pleasanter way to live. You become more and more emotionally mature, navigating natural consequences that help you "right" your path. You look beyond the surface for the truth of yourself, of the situation, of everyone you meet, of every encounter you have.

Say you encounter a friend who is condescending to you. Instead of lamenting that maybe you were wrong, you recognize the friend's behavior is not for you. It feels wrong, so it is wrong for you. Therefore, as we discussed in the last chapter, the relationship is not for you, which might lead you to choose to hold a boundary with that friend. Setting a boundary serves two purposes: One, you are giving this friend a way to come back to their own knowing and person. And two, you are able to stay with yourself instead of stepping back into The Model by overthinking what happened and who is right or wrong. The situation either works for you or it doesn't. A friend who belongs in your life doesn't treat you poorly. An aligned friend clearly states who they can and cannot be. "I'm feeling poorly today, and I need 'X' support," or "I'm not able to spend time together today; can we reschedule?" These are friends who are responsive to themselves and therefore to you too.

This is not to say we have to cut everybody out of our life. We just have to make sure we prioritize making room in our life for ourselves. We have to make sure that at this growth moment, we work with our knowing, so we attract the people who really understand us and who we've likely spent our lifetime looking for. Know, however, that there's a good reason we haven't been with them. We first need to see what isn't working in our lives and create change for ourselves before we can attract such people. And if you're an HSP, remember feeling different now makes you able to see what is missing and create needed change.

The very nature of knowing embodies integrity, therefore what is shared is profound for those attracted to it, with or without understanding that attraction. Not a stroke of the ego but a validation that you are on the right path for you. Eventually, your curiosity leads you to situations where you find other people who are also emotionally mature, people who can see and hear you. This cannot be rushed. You cannot go out in the world with this concept before you are ready to receive it. But you can begin to exercise your curiosity whenever you feel judgment coming on. You can allow repetition and intense desire to outrun everything society has told you is "good" and replace it with confidence in what works for you. You can replace it with a life that lets you shine and shines as an example for the world.

TRUST IN YOU

It is normal for those of us who have lived in a culture devoted to The Model to feel hesitant about our knowing and letting it guide us in our decision-making. I was afraid of my own abilities until my late twenties when I felt so confined by the life I was living that I could not help but challenge The Model–like assumptions that had landed me there. My guess is that is what you are feeling now and probably have been for some time. My guess is also that as you read through each chapter of this book, you felt relief, understood, and I hope you feel seen.

Through challenging The Model and my own self-questioning over the years, I came to re-know my power. I came to understand that there is no upper hand whatsoever above what I know is true. There only needs to be a relationship to our power. While sometimes easy and sometimes scary, trusting in yourself and your knowing is the only way back to being fully yourself. Unlike living in The Model, our knowing promises nothing. No high ideals. Only humanness. In our knowing, there is no hierarchy of ability or importance—simply your way and my way. Though in time, there will be our ways together, making room for the world to operate in a far different way than it does today—a more natural way to who we are as humans.

When you live that trust, you live a passionate, calm, and confident life, which is our nature as humans; not an ideal to uphold. You live a life that you know and choose, not that others have chosen for you. You have no need to control or posture. Your shadow is released. You evolve to find the people, places, and opportunities that offer no limit to your expression and expansion. You live sure that in every second, you are where you need to be—and you feel it. Uninhibited, you are in the flow, moving your unique self toward realizing your full potential. You thrive.

My desire is that we all thrive. That we come to trust in ourselves and live guided by our knowing. I want every doctor to have a 100 percent success rate, every mother to feel supported in her choices for her children, every child to feel free to live out their own form of echolocation, and all of us to push ourselves to the limit of our potential—because that is indeed who we are. That is who you are. That is what makes our world heal and what restores our nature as humans. That is what is ours when we live by our knowing.

Now that you know, you have what you need to find your way back to yourself and restore your personal knowing. You now know that you have it within you to explore the world as only you can through a cultivated expression of who you are through a healed standpoint. I know you feel this inside. It is time to let it show—to live it—on the outside. You will want for nothing, and on this, everything arrives. You can do this because you want to do this—and because I know, and you know that you must.

ACKNOWLEDGMENTS

There are many people in my life who played necessary, while challenging, roles for me. I consider them my greatest teachers, but none more so than my mother, who played a role I never could. Her success at creating such deep contrast for so many, including me, tells me of her profound ability to love "on the other side." Out of this personal experience grew a complexity that took me decades to unfurl and understand for myself, which now informs this book. I also know there are two sides to relating, and I'm sorry for any hurt I may have caused others in the process and hope it ultimately helped you to grow as well.

Thank you to the many clients who informed these pages and the stages of restoring ourselves and why that is important in today's world. Your strife was heard. You granted me a multitude of situations on which to apply what I could see, and as a result, build upon in understanding my work. Your situations live on through my work and lay a foundational example for those who read these pages.

Thank you to my editor, who challenged me and taught me the process of writing a book. This was a massive learning curve for me.

You've helped me become a better writer, seeing where to let go in writing and where to claim my voice most fully. Your support was invaluable.

Thank you to those I met while traveling these last few years. Some of you extended more love to me than I'd ever experienced, showing me I was on the path to finding where I belonged and signaling it was safe to "come home" within myself.

Thank you to my friends who counseled me through tough moments and let me lean on their intuition. When I returned to the United States, you gave me a soft landing while fully supporting and understanding my need to travel. Thanks in particular to all of you who said independently and unsolicited, "I see you as running to, not from." Thank you for seeing me.

To the founding members of the Wisdom Gathering, thank you. Your dedication, tenacity, audacity, and wild desire for true freedom within are constant reminders of why I do the work I do.

Lastly, to my children: You were the silent catalyst for everything I've achieved. You were the constant I needed to champion how to parent you altogether differently, learn about intuition in a drama-free and powerful way, keep myself afloat during healing from chronic Lyme disease, and step forward into the unknown to empower myself and become the example of the greatest level of expansion I can achieve. Thank you for your influence on my life; your ways of thinking and acting are extraordinary. Thanks to you both for being exactly who you are.

ABOUT THE AUTHOR

AMY CERNY VASTERLING is a future-focused public speaker, author, teacher, and intuitive sharing the importance of returning to your personal knowing. Her unique perspective honed over several decades shows what people refer to as "narcissism" as a high-level social disordering. Like with any desire for change, something needs to displace the old. In this case she has found it is our expression, which is often hampered by judgment, that leads to control. Amy observed the recurrence of people's aim to tell others "I know better for you than you know for yourself" and realized this was a key to the full story of the insecurity behind it all. Amy believes humanity has a great future as we mature emotionally and leave something she calls The Model behind. Now she empowers individuals and communities to dynamically return to the truth of who they are so they can restore human connection, find where they truly belong, and fully live life.

www.ingramcontent.com/pod-product-compliance
Lightning Source LLC
Chambersburg PA
CBHW031415120626
46545CB00006B/2143